How to

Overcome

Barriers

to Growth

and Bring

New Life

to an

Established

Church

TURN-AROUND CHURCHES

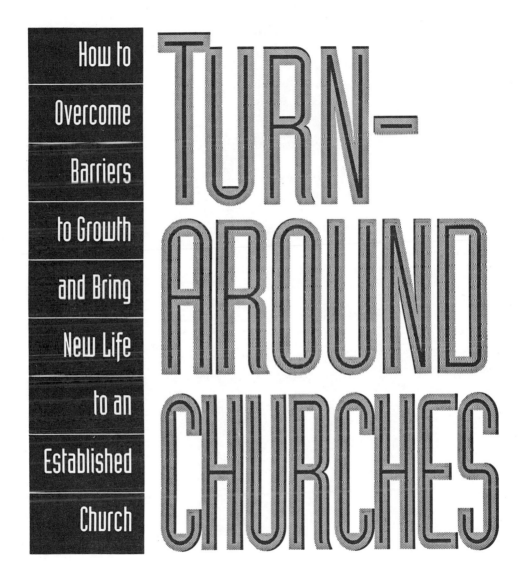

GEORGE BARNA

Author of THE FROG IN THE KETTLE and THE POWER OF VISION

How to
Overcome
Barriers
to Growth
and Bring
New Life
to an
Established
Church

TURN-AROUND CHURCHES

Regal Books
A Division of Gospel Light
Ventura, California, U.S.A.

Published by Regal Books
A Division of Gospel Light
Ventura, California, U.S.A.
Printed in U.S.A.

Library of Congress Cataloging-in-Publication Data
Barna, George.
    Turnaround churches : how to overcome barriers to growth and bring new life to an established church / George Barna.
        p. cm.
    ISBN 0-8307-1592-4
    1. Church renewal. 2. Pastoral theology. I. Title.
BV600.2.B34 1993
254'.5—dc20
                                                        93-31864
                                                             CIP

1 2 3 4 5 6 7 8 9 10 11 12 / Q3.11 / KP / 00 99 98 97 96 95 94 93

Rights for publishing this book in other languages are contracted by Gospel Literature International (GLINT). GLINT also provides technical help for the adaptation, translation and publishing of Bible study resources and books in scores of languages worldwide. For further information, contact GLINT, P.O. Box 4060, Ontario, CA 91761-1003, U.S.A., or the publisher.

Contents

A presentation of principles rather than statistics or models on how to turn around a dying church, and how a healthy church can cope with changes that affect its growth and ministry.

Protestant churches experience a life cycle similar to that of businesses, and should be aware that maturity brings problems that may need fixing to avoid a downward spiral and a declining ministry.

A study of 30 turnaround churches revealed that a number of symptoms usually contribute to a church's decline. This chapter offers a list of eight areas to check in diagnosing a congregation's state of health.

Interviews identified 11 factors that were present when a dying church was restored to wholeness, ranging from replacing the pastor to reliance on the Holy Spirit, and widespread and heartfelt prayer.

Acknowledgments

HERE IS A SALUTE TO MY ACCOMPLICES ON THIS ADVENTURE.

Gwen Ingram deserves a mountain of credit for her work on this project. She scouted the churches that might qualify for the project, screened them, conducted the interviews, typed the transcript of each interview for my use and shared the audiotapes of the conversations. It was a pleasure to see her grow more excited about the research as the project developed.

My colleagues at Barna Research have, as usual, continued the work of the organization while I generated the text for this book. Thanks are due to a great group of professionals who make projects such as this possible: Jeff Blake, Salvina Cappello, Cindy Coats, Vibeke Klocke, George Maupin, Paul Rottler, Diane Swartz and Telford Work.

My wife and daughter, Nancy and Samantha, were instrumental in this process, too. They prayed for me, listened patiently to my complaints about timelines and pressures, expressed (or convincingly feigned) interest in the work and encouraged me to do the best job I could do. My wife read early versions of several chapters and provided brutally honest, but vitally useful, criticism. She and my daughter are an indispensable part of my efforts. I love them and appreciate them.

My friends at Gospel Light performed their duties related to this book with their typical high-intensity level of support and encouragement. Bill Greig III, Bill Greig Jr., Gary Greig, Kyle Duncan, Virginia Woodard, Bill Denzel, Terry Donnelly, Nola Grunden, Barbara Fisher, Gloria Moss, Dennis Somers and the rest of the staff that make these projects work so smoothly are again extended my sincerest thanks. It is truly a blessing to labor alongside such saints.

Perhaps the most important people were the pastors we interviewed and whose churches we studied. Without their generous gifts of time and related resources, this project would still be merely a concept. They are busy people who shared their time, energy and experiences for the good of the Kingdom. May their sacrifice bear much fruit in the Lord's vineyard.

On behalf of all these people, and for the glory of God, I pray that this book will help ministries across the nation bring more people into God's presence, into community with other believers and into wholehearted, effective service of the only One who counts.

Introduction

FOR NEARLY A CENTURY, THE ESTEEMED SEARS CATALOG REIGNED AS THE SYMBOL of mail-order marketing. When that marketing resource was initiated in 1894, it addressed a great need: satisfying the product desires of people located too distant from a Sears store to conveniently acquire the product, given that most Americans lacked easy transportation to the Sears retail establishments.

Over the course of its existence, tens of millions of people purchased items through the catalog, helping to lift Sears to the top of the retail universe.

Using relatively little fanfare, however, the retail giant announced in early 1993 that the catalog would cease to be published. Indeed, the catalog was now a historical relic for Sears, an indication that what worked well in one cultural context was not guaranteed a similar level of success in a different context. Not even 95 years of stellar service to a nation's consumers could protect the existence of the entity.

More than a few of us recognized the irony in the situation: the grandfather of direct-marketing catalogs was being buried at the very time when direct marketing was experiencing unprecedented success and growth in the American marketplace. Direct marketing is now a $90 billion business each year. When Sears introduced its catalog, sales through direct marketing were less than $10 million annually nationwide.

The death of this venerable marketing mechanism was an indisputable signal of the monumental changes revolutionizing the marketplace. What was once the envy of the marketing world had become a millstone around Sears' neck. The only wise decision for Sears to make was to put an end to its catalog sales. What was once the company's glowing strength had become its glaring weakness.

LEADERSHIP KEYED TO CHRYSLER'S SUCCESS

A different type of change had swept through the Chrysler Corporation during the 15-year tenure of Lee Iacocca. The cigar-smoking, tough-talking chief executive of America's number three automaker became a major celebrity in America during the '80s, probably emerging as the nation's best-known business executive.

This notoriety was earned when the former Ford Motor Company executive took the reigns of the faltering car manufacturer and not only rescued it from the brink of bankruptcy (i.e., ensuring survival), but also built a relatively solid base for the future of the company (i.e., modest success).

Opinions about Iacocca, the man, are as varied as the price range of Chrysler's stock over the past two decades. Most memorable about the Chrysler story was the fact that a dead company was resuscitated under a dynamic leader who had a defined, well-articulated vision for his organization and had the drive and skills to bring that future to pass. In a nation starved for strong and effective leadership, people forgave the idiosyncrasies of the man in light of his ability to perform as a strong leader.

These are just two of the numerous examples of how organizations have coped with dramatic cultural and demographic changes that have reshaped the environment in which they operate.

Coping with Change

Starting from a position of strength as Sears and Chrysler did before their dissipation, certainly does not guarantee or even facilitate long-term, enduring success in a marketplace transformed by a breadth of changes. Even as the environment in which these organizations operate has changed, so must the organizations themselves adapt to these changes without losing their vision, distinctions and core values.

REALITY AND THE CHURCH

All of this raises some interesting questions for churches. You have undoubtedly encountered—firsthand, through reading or in conversation—stories of churches that have attempted to cope with change.

Most Churches Tinker with Change

Some churches attempt to change by ignoring changes in the ministry context. Others gravitate to the other end of the spectrum and essentially reinvent themselves, creating a new ministry while attempting to adapt to change.

Most churches reside between these two extremes. They are aware of changes taking place around them, tinkering here and there with policies, programs, perspectives and personnel just enough to get by without having to radically revisit their philosophy of ministry or their processes for ministry.

By far the most alluring stories, of course, are those that capture our imagination with anecdotes and snippets of reality drawn from the explosive growth of unknown congregations, which, often virtually overnight, became megachurches.

A few of the well-known "models" for growth are Willow Creek Community Church in Barrington, Illinois; Saddleback Community Church in Mission Viejo, California; Skyline Wesleyan Church in Lemon Grove, California; Community Church of Joy in Phoenix, Arizona; Perimeter Church in Atlanta, Georgia; and The Church On The Way in Van Nuys, California.

Indeed, thousands of churches across America are growing numerically and spiritually, and consequently are leaving a positive impact on the communities they serve.

Study and Adaptation Are Essential

Typically, I find that the pastors of such megachurches attribute a significant part of that impact and growth to studying the ministry terrain and to adapting their ministry practices to the needs and realities of the community context without undermining their theological

While many churches grow, other congregations pursue business as though they were living during the days of their grandfathers.

beliefs. (No, they do not leave God out of the equation. They invariably identify God's blessing and other spiritual factors as central to their growth and development.)

While we have a few thousand large and growing churches dotting the map, many more Protestant churches and denominations have chosen to pursue business as usual as if they were ministering in the context faced by their grandfathers.

The outcome of this mind-set and the associated behavior is frequently disastrous. Rather than learn or take cues from the experience and wisdom of direct marketers, mass marketers, franchisers, market analysts and church colleagues, many professional clergy have chosen to follow the models of ministry that were popular centuries ago.

THE FLIP SIDE OF SUCCESS

To do ourselves justice in the practice of ministry, we must be willing to ask some tough questions.

For instance, in spite of all the books about church dynamics, the many seminaries that explore and expound on ministry issues and the numerous studies conducted in relation to church life, how much do we really know about why churches grow or decline; why some churches succeed while some fail; why so many churches fail to reach their initial potential while other churches far exceed anyone's wildest dreams?

Failure Is Not a Popular Subject

Over the years, bits and pieces of research have been conducted to ascertain the dynamics of church growth. Surprisingly, considerably less exploration has been made of the dynamics of church decline or deterioration. If you have any doubts, visit a Christian bookstore and ask to see the books related to church growth. In a well-stocked store, you will have access to more than 50 titles. Then ask to examine the volumes related to church decline. By stretching the definition, perhaps you will have a handful of books to evaluate.

One of our natural tendencies as Americans is to focus on success. We publish magazines and books every month on how to achieve success. We esteem those people who reflect a tangible degree of success in their chosen walk of life. We have evolved into a statistics-crazed society, partly because of our obsession with the identification of success.

What seems to have remained a rather well-kept secret is that failure often served as the object of study by people who ultimately rose to success. I am not suggesting that life is a zero sum game, that is, for every failure there is a success of equal proportions.

The Study of Failure Is Often Helpful

Yet, ample evidence exists to hypothesize that the people and organizations that have the greatest chance of success are those that have recognized and intentionally addressed potential pitfalls by building on the insights and adventures of their predecessors. In other words, unless we study our failures, we are destined to repeat them. And, repeat them the Protestant church in America has!

The national landscape is littered with churches that have done their best to develop a strong and important ministry center, only to find after a period of years that the resulting church has made little real progress toward reaching its goals in serving God. Our investigation of such ministries suggests that while good intentions permeated these churches, wisdom in the sense of studying failures and successes in relevant contexts was absent.

This book is a modest attempt to provide a systematic study of why churches fail and how some of these dying ministries were revived and brought back to a glorious state of health.

Two Sides of the Equation

In these pages, I hope to share with you not only the disaster side of the equation (what caused the decline of a group of strong churches), but also the encouraging side of the equation (how these churches were able to step back from the brink of extinction).

This book may be a road map to recovery, and it can identify pitfalls that could put healthy churches "on the ropes."

Without being unreasonably optimistic about the chances of a once-healthy church being turned around after a severe decline, our research demonstrates that there is relatively little reason for such optimism.

It is hoped that this book will paint a portrait of how such a turnaround might be effected. If you are connected to a church experiencing a serious decline, perhaps this volume will provide a road map for recovery.

This book is not intended only for those who have a church that is "on the ropes." During the last several years, I have worked with and have studied numerous churches. One thing I have discovered is that leaders of stable or growing churches generally have an interest in identifying the pitfalls that could lead to the demise of their congregations and in learning how to sense and to avoid them.

If you are connected to a congregation that is stable or growing and have an interest in protecting the future development of that church, perhaps this book can be used profitably as a dose of preventive medicine.

CHURCH TURNAROUND POSSIBLE

As you read this book, be prepared for some principles that you may expect, but also for some insights that may surprise you. Be prepared for some tough realities—the types of discoveries that may not seem very encouraging but that are the harsh realities we must address if we are serious about serving God with diligence, intelligence and excellence.

Turnaround Pastors Are Rare

In our research, we discovered some factors pertaining to the type of person who can turn a church around and have concluded that those pastors are rare.

We learned some information about the most critical first steps for a pastor to take in turning a church around, and some of the most important steps are unrelated to growth techniques or strategic planning.

The study unfolded insights into what types of congregations have the potential to be turned around. In many cases, trying to revitalize a declining church is probably a wasted effort.

The death of a church is usually avoidable, but it may take a different type of ministry mind-set than many of today's church leaders possess.

Making Lives More Christlike

The intent of this book, of course, is not to shock, to amaze or to belittle the reader. The purpose is to inform leaders so that churches can be more effective mechanisms for transforming people's lives toward Christlikeness.

If, in the process, we stumble onto some truths that break from the conventional line of thought or provide some insights into ourselves and the nature of ministry, so much the better. Nothing is inherently wrong with the "business" of ministry being intriguing or compelling.

The Church, of course, was never intended by Christ to be a technique-driven institution. His call was for believers to band together in ways that built a unified family of saints dedicated to becoming more like Him.

We found that turnaround churches were more committed to Jesus and His people than to procedures or to other systematic responses to challenge.

In the end, we found that turnaround churches were more committed to Jesus and His people than to procedures or to other systematic responses to a challenging situation. Exactly how these churches exhibit their love for, and pursuit of, the Master is often a heartwarming, encouraging return to the basics of biblical ministry.

A WORD ABOUT RESEARCH

Typically, Barna Research conducts quantitative studies, that is, research based upon a projectable national sample. This study, much like that underlying the content of *User Friendly Churches*, is qualitative, which means that this study does not provide statistics that can be projected to the aggregate church population.

Thirty Churches Were Studied
Using a "snowball sample," that is, contacting denominations, turnaround churches, publishers, research and consulting groups, and other observers of the church scene for referrals drawn from personal experience, we identified a list of churches that at one time had been

thriving congregations, then experienced a steep decline but ultimately pulled out of the dive and became revitalized.

We contacted the pastors of these churches, screened them to be sure they fit this profile and conducted lengthy open-ended interviews of one to two hours with each of them. Documents provided to us by these pastors helped to describe the revitalization process that had taken place. Eventually, we based this book on 30 turnaround churches in 16 states. Church size ranged from a current attendance of 135 to 3,300.

A sample of this size is certainly not large enough to claim that the resulting findings provide a comprehensive insight into the turnaround process. However, in striving to find such churches, we learned another key lesson: When a church takes a nosedive in attendance or membership, it generally does not make a comeback.

Chance of Success Is Slim
The typical experience seems to be that, once a church loses its momentum, the most probable outcome is either death or stabilization at a much smaller size.

A major reason why I agreed to work with this relatively small sample is that, although the universe of turnaround churches is undoubtedly much larger than our sample, it is a relatively small universe overall. The church observers with whom we worked in developing the sample confirmed this to be an accurate perception based on their experience.

The churches represent all geographic parts of the country, a wide variety of Protestant denominations and a considerable range in the size of congregations. The appendix provides information on the geographic distribution of the churches and other background characteristics.

The names and locations of the churches are not included in the text to protect the pastors from the deluge of contacts that normally result when a "model" for a particular process is described in print.

The purpose of this book, after all, is to help distill the experiences of a number of turnaround churches toward developing a body of knowledge on this topic that transcends the history of a single church.

Solutions Unique to Each Church

The decision not to identify the churches (although I do use the names of pastors) stems from a great frustration of mine: the tendency to engage in ministry by mimicry. Because every church is unique in its context, its resources, its strengths and weaknesses and its opportunities, every church must develop its own unique solutions to its circumstances.

While copying what others have done is easier than creating a novel and contextualized response, it is rarely effective. I would rather assist leaders in understanding the transferable principles from the experiences of a range of churches than to be party to enabling a church to duplicate the responses of a specific church, no matter how brilliant or effective the work of the turnaround church might have been.

Principles, Not Statistics, Are Stressed

The text, then, provides a narrative of the principles rather than a series of statistics or models. Based on what we discovered through this research, I hope to provide insights that will either help you turn around a frail church or to prevent a major slide in a church that is presently strong.

I believe the prescriptions for healthy ministry contained in these pages are strong medicine, but lesser remedies appear unable to turn around churches that are critically ill.

Reshaping the Life Cycle

FOUR DECADES AGO, BUSINESS ANALYSTS RECOGNIZED A DISCERNIBLE PATTERN TO the life of most organizations. The pattern, generally described as a life cycle, is defined by four stages: birth, development, maturity and decline.

Recent research has provided insight into some common reasons for passage from one stage to another and offers some clues about how long an organization is likely to thrive, based upon its internal culture, behavior and processes.

But one of the realities the traditional life cycle does not take into account is the experience of those organizations that have reached maturity (i.e., "success") followed by a rapid, free-fall decline, succeeded by a near-miraculous full recovery to balanced maturity. This capacity to turn around a severely ailing organization is quite rare; bankruptcy or closing the doors forever are the more typical outcomes.

CHURCHES AS A MICROCOSM

The Protestant churches in our nation provide a wonderful microcosm for evaluating the life cycle process. Although their motive for existence is not financial profit, they live or die by the same basic set of organizational principles as do the McDonald's restaurants, IBMs and Exxons of the world.

What we learn from the research conducted on and among these giant profit-making entities can be applied to the life of the local church. Similarly, the lessons emerging from church crises can help other organizations mature more efficiently.

Four Organizational Stages

In studying the behavior of churches, the four typical stages of organizational life are readily apparent. It is common to find a newly planted church bursting with energy and enthusiasm in its early years.

Born from a common need among a group of people with identical or complementary goals, the daunting realities of creating a new church seem more like an attractive challenge than an overwhelming, odds-are-against-us barrier. What these ministries lack in sophistication they tend to make up for in passion and determination. In

Many people who are attracted to a new church have a pioneer spirit and wish to find opportunities to stretch their giftedness.

speaking with many pastors over the years, we have often heard wistful comments about the naive joy of ministry in the early years.

Many of the people drawn to a new church have a pioneer spirit. They are driven to make something special happen and to stamp the new ministry with their personalities and dreams of adding to the kingdom of God. Playing a founding role in the development of a new congregation is fancied to be not only a positive spiritual adventure, but also a practical opportunity to stretch a person's spiritual journey and giftedness.

After a church is established and the ministry is functioning, the spiritual battle kicks into gear and the church slowly loses some of its childlikeness. As the initial euphoria of establishing the church wears off, members of the congregation become more cognizant of conditions and circumstances that previously had been outside their conscious consideration or focus.

In this developmental stage, the church typically loses some of the entrepreneurial innocence and starts to become more set in its ways. At this point the church generally institutes a relatively predictable series of programs and policies and confronts the perplexities of facilities and infrastructure. The zeal that initially was focused on ministry and the personal touch—that is, the "why" and "who" of ministry—now concentrates upon how ministry is done.

After some years of working through such issues, the church has reached its mature stage: the people, practices, policies, perspectives and places are firmly established. Change may still be introduced on a regular basis, but the foundations of the ministry have been solidified and the future of the church almost immutably has been shaped by these decisions.

When a mature church accepts change, it tends to be incremental rather than revolutionary in nature. The church now has discernible traditions, people who reign as the "pillars" and systems that were developed to allow ministry, but simultaneously serve to limit, if not to prevent, innovation and rapid response to opportunities.

Many Rest on a Plateau

This is the plateau on which most churches rest for many years. It is a period of tremendous vulnerability for the church in spite of the complacency and sense of comfort that such maturity brings.

This danger exists because the dominant motivation that undergirded the initiation of the ministry has dissipated (i.e., a heart to change the world for Christ in unique and effective ways). The smugness that comes with maturity often spells the first step of decline for a church, regardless of its membership size, the magnitude of the annual budget or the church's physical plant.

Consequently, many churches enter the fourth and final phase of the life cycle quietly, perhaps fully unaware that they have begun a slow descent into ministry oblivion. A number of telltale signs start to show.

The zealous people who initially carried the church—those who represented the ministry heart and passion—lose their aggressiveness for Christ and His purposes or depart for new churches as they recognize that the structures now in place inhibit rather than encourage ministry intensity.

The mechanics of ministry, in particular, have an entirely different focus. The budget becomes reshaped to coincide with redirected priorities and concerns: Less money actually goes to ministry, more to overhead.

The number of people on staff grows while the lay involvement in hands-on ministry shrinks. Fewer and fewer visitors come—and stay—causing a slow reduction in the attendance at key church events and programs.

Sometimes this final phase approaches like a tornado. In some cases, it is caused by scandal within the church: the moral failure of the pastor, the misappropriation of church funds, a personality conflict between key leaders that leads to a split and so on.

Occasionally, the rapid demise is facilitated by the pastor leaving the church to assume similar duties at another congregation. In "personality churches," once the pastor leaves, the church is without a star performer and, having no roots in community or ministry, the church falls apart.

In other cases, the opening of a new church in the vicinity or the presence of one having a charismatic pastor may be enough to bleed much of the remaining life from a church that is mature in age but not in spirituality.

Death Is the Usual Outcome

As is true in the business world, when a church experiences a period of intense hemorrhaging, death is the usual outcome. Of course, because churches are nonprofit entities whose existence requires only a name and a person or two to maintain the legacy, a dead church is not necessarily an ex-church.

Thousands of churches across America have deteriorated to the point where they are a ministry in theory only, a shell of what they had once been. In these churches, little, if any, outreach or inreach takes place. The name and buildings may insinuate a church is present, but lives are not touched in a significant, spiritual way by such artifacts. As long as these churches have a handful of faithful attenders and can afford some

---

The good news is that some churches can reverse a rapid decline and make a full comeback to health.

---

meeting space and a speaker, they remain in existence. They have, however, essentially completed their life as a church.

The good news is that some churches experience a rapid decline but are able to end that hemorrhaging and make a full comeback to healthy Christian ministry. These are referred to as turnaround churches, and they are the exceptions to the rule.

It is valuable, however, to understand their experience well enough to discover the principles underlying the turnaround, which can enable other churches to avoid the same pitfalls that necessitated the comeback or to enable dying churches to turn around.

SURVIVING A TAILSPIN

Bill Cochrane had been pastor of his church for seven years when he noticed that things just were not going right.

"I remember sitting in my study one afternoon, kind of daydreaming about what I had envisioned the church becoming with me at the helm," Cochrane said. "And suddenly the light went on in my head, and I recognized that we were regressing, not progressing. Nothing drastic, mind you, just a steady loss of members, money and spirit.

"Over the next few weeks I started to explore the decline more thoroughly and was able to confirm its existence, but not what caused it and certainly not what I could do about it."

Collapse Took Five Years

Cochrane's church attendance continued to decline from a peak of about 400 people in regular attendance at worship services to 50 to 75. This collapse took about five years to occur. It weighed heavily on him.

"I never felt so helpless and so frustrated in all my life," Cochrane said. "I had devoted myself to the church, as best I knew how, but it wasn't working. My sermons were okay, not world class, but nothing that should cause people to leave in droves. The programs were adequate, I suppose, but we had lost the fire.

"Frankly, I was so discouraged once I saw what was happening and felt it was beyond my control that I just didn't have the umph left to rekindle the flame. Like many in the church, I guess I gave up. It hadn't even occurred to me that one reason the numbers were down was because everybody but me knew that we were on the decline."

Cochrane said that many church people, especially the less committed ones, left at the first sign of decline. The realization of what was happening was a crushing blow, he said.

"That's when I handed in my resignation. I still believed in the people and knew there was great potential. But I also knew they'd be better off with a new pastor. I certainly wasn't doing them any favors by staying around."

Jack Szykowski was an elder in the church and had been for 15 years at the time of Cochrane's departure. He had been there when the church had its "glory days" and had stuck with it through the decline.

"It was awful," Szykowski said. "People were discouraged. Leaders in the church stopped serving. The church wasn't fun anymore. It was almost like people could smell failure bearing down on us and wanted to run away from it as fast as they could. Not get associated with that failure, you know?

"What really rattled my cage was the hypocrisy of it all. Here we'd been talking for some years about community and love and bearing each other's burdens. Then, when the going got tough, everyone got going—out the back door—because it was tough. No community, no bonds of faith.

"Today, this church is just a skeleton of what it was," Szykowski said, "and I keep asking myself if all the sacrifice I put into it was really worth it. Because, when Christianity is real, you see it in behavior, not just words. And I don't see the fruit of 15 years of labor."

A member of the shrunken congregation, Muriel Forrester, talked softly about her experience at the church, and where it is at today.

"Sometimes I wake up on Sunday mornings and just lay there thinking I must be crazy to keep attending that church," she said. "The pastor left. The people left. The leaders gave up. Why am I sticking with it? I don't even know what hit us, or what happened to all the people. It just seemed like one day we were happy, singing, praying together, and the next day it was like a funeral parlor. No scandals or fights, just a steady loss of people. So discouraging.

"Oh, I tell you, it burns me up to even think about it. But what's the point of getting angry? That's just people, our fallen nature, I suppose. But I have to admit, even with the new pastor—he's a nice young fellow, right out of seminary—I don't get excited about the church like I used to."

Theirs is not a unique story. Pastors, leaders and congregants typically experience pain and anxiety from being part of a church that falls apart. Pastors often voice doubts about their capacity to minister, confusion over God's will for their life and ministry, and disappointment at having let down so many people.

Lay leaders express remorse at what may have been wasted time and effort and at their inability to be more effective in building a strong foundation. They also express fear regarding involvement in further service. Members feel cheated or abandoned. About the only people who seem relatively unscathed by the experience are those who jumped ship early and either joined another, more dynamic ministry or no longer attend a church.

From Rags to Riches

But the stories of the people involved in churches that were on the downward spiral and made a dramatic comeback are inspiring.

Phil Thomason led one church out of the death spiral. Under a predecessor, the regular Sunday church attendance had dropped from more than 600 people to barely 200. Thomason, whose only experience was as an associate pastor, accepted the challenge fully aware of the minefield into which he was stepping.

"But somehow this seemed like the place God wanted me," Thomason said, "and I sensed a spark of interest in the remaining core of people to rebuild what had once been a strong ministry. If this was a straight business decision, a wise executive would have explored the options and said, 'No thanks.'" But if God is at the center of the decision-making process, and you really feel His call, the worldly criteria are less important.

Wounded Church Recovers

In his mid-30s when he took the church, Thomason felt this wounded church offered a good environment for exercising many of the skills he had developed earlier in life but could not utilize fully as an associate.

"I love a good challenge," Thomason said. "I didn't realize then just how huge a challenge the turnaround process is. Honestly, if I had any inkling of what it has taken to revitalize this church, I either would have been scared away or simply said that nobody has what it takes to make it happen. Truly it's been by the grace of God that this church has come back to life."

Alexis Federico, a church member for a decade, said, "I can't tell you how exciting it has been to be here during this rebuilding period. The pastor has done a remarkable job, but the people have really made it happen.

"People come here expecting God to do great things now. It wasn't like that before the pastor came. We kept watching as the church we knew and loved disappeared before our eyes. But God has used Pastor Phil to restore our confidence in God and in ourselves. We know God will bless this work, and we're anxious to be a part of that and to see how He'll do it."

The same degree of enthusiasm was evident in the comments of Carl Jenkins, a church elder. "I tell you, going through something like this either drums you out of the church altogether or it restores your faith in God. You just have to believe in miracles after an experience like this.

"And the great thing is that He's not done with us yet! We know that we will continue to grow and mature and make a difference in this community. After this kind of return, we sometimes get to feeling invincible, like there's nothing that can stop us now. We're alive and looking for real ways to touch the world."

Jenkins sheepishly admits that during the crisis period at the church, he, like many others, was tempted to give in and to drift off to another church where ministry was less taxing. He persevered, how-

We're growing because there's a new vital-ity here that's attracting folks who never had time for God.

ever, and asserts that he is more excited about ministry as a result of having lived through the hard times to see God at work.

"We're not just growing because we attracted the old members back," he said. "We're growing because there's a new vitality here that's attracting folks who never had time for God. We're getting people who always thought they could wait till they were on their deathbed to deal with religion."

Church Is Now the Place to Be

Typical of those who pour themselves into a turnaround that is successful, Jenkins said, "Yes sir, this church is the place to be now. It's exciting to see lives being turned around, just as this church has been turned around. God worked through some very special people to make this change happen."

When Raul Mendoza moved into an apartment near the church, he contemplated visiting a church as a way of getting acquainted with the community and to meet some people. However, Mendoza was hesitant to take the step because churches he had attended while growing up were "pretty boring and meaningless."

Mendoza mentioned his dilemma at lunch one day to a few of his friends. He was not prepared for the enthusiasm two of his coworkers displayed regarding the church they attended. In short order they persuaded him to try Pastor Thomason's church.

"I thought, *hey, what the heck, Catholic church, Baptist church, it's all just church; I'll go and make the guys happy.* But I was really surprised when I went there. It was so different. There was a lot of energy, a real sense of warmth and purpose. It wasn't just church for the sake of church. It was more real."

In a culture that increasingly questions the wisdom of devoting time and other resources to church life, involvement in ministry is an intentional and significant decision.

Mendoza is cautiously optimistic about the church and his connection there. "I don't know how to describe it really. It has become a part of my weekly routine. I'm meeting people, learning things from the Bible, even thinking about getting involved in some of the programs they have. Yeah, it's quite a change for me, but I like it."

A New Spin on Church

In the turnaround churches, it is common to hear the people involved speak with great joy about the hope that has been rekindled in and by their church. They credit their pastor and leaders with doing good work, but are awestruck by what God has chosen to do to and through the church.

These churches frequently are among the most evangelistic, service-oriented congregations in their area. As is true at almost any church that is modeling the Acts 2 experience of believers committing their lives to Christ and to each other, it is encouraging and exciting to be in their midst.

Clearly, people are affected by the health of the church they attend. In a culture that increasingly questions the wisdom of devoting time and other resources to church life, involvement in ministry is an intentional and significant decision. To become attached to a church that undergoes an agonizing decline can have a life-changing impact—and usually not for the better. Understanding the dynamics of this process can help each of us who are involved with a local church be better prepared and skilled to address the potential demise of our own churches.

Business analysts have a popular saying: "If it ain't broke, don't fix it." In the pages that follow, we will explore how God has worked to repair some churches that were broken and how those that are not yet broken might avoid falling into disrepair.

The Symptoms of Decline

WHEN I WAS YOUNG, I VISITED A DOCTOR TO DETERMINE THE CAUSE OF A PAR-ticularly painful throat infection. As the examination progressed, it became clear to me that the doctor was taking more than the usual amount of time and was finding nothing that would enlighten the family about my condition. To ease the tension, I ventured that probably nothing was wrong with me. In a patient, grandfatherly way, he assured me that *something* was irritating my larynx.

"There's always a cause," the doctor said. "Unfortunately, even when we know where the pain is, we sometimes don't know what to look for."

Many churches struggle with the same paradox: Even when they sense something is wrong, they don't know what to look for.

Our research found that some churches were well into the throes of their decline before they realized their desperate situation, and at that point it was too late to do much but ride it out. Other churches knew a problem was at hand but could not identify its nature.

THE NATURE OF DECLINE

Even in the limited number of churches we studied, four crucial insights into the nature of the decline were identified.

The List Is Limitless
First, it appears that the list of catalysts underlying a collapse is virtually limitless. Some of the reasons identified were common to many of these churches, such as shifting demographics in the ministry area and a pastor who no longer was able to lead the church.

Other reasons were idiosyncratic, such as one church's day school problems that undermined its community image, or another church that unknowingly hired a radical feminist staff person who ultimately split the congregation.

The problems causing a church decline are no respecters of boundaries. They relate to people, programs, facilities, theology, finances and style of ministry.

No Single Factor to Blame
Second, none of the churches could blame the decline on a single factor. In every situation we explored, the church was suffering from two or more harmful conditions.

It seems that in all but the most extraordinary of cases, a truly healthy church will not fall apart due to a single catastrophic element. It takes more than one Achilles' heel to bring down the typical church. But when two or more diseases are present, the church frequently will enter a tailspin that requires immediate and radical response to prevent a severe decline.

Some Problems Are Universal
Third, most of the churches we evaluated experienced several identical problems. The ways these elements came about differed, the combination of plagues visited upon the church varied and the relative significance of each element within the collapse of a given church was unique.

However, this handful of symptoms was notable for their consistent presence among the churches suffering from near-terminal crises.

Finally, it is apparent that with proper attention and response, all of these debilitating factors are avoidable. Sidestepping these challenges is no easy task, but it is possible.

EIGHT SYMPTOMS TO WATCH

Think objectively about your church for a moment and identify some of the difficulties it faces. How many of the following, life-threatening difficulties are confronting your church today?

Demographic Changes

Few communities remain static over the course of time. Every year almost one-fifth of the nation's population moves. Nearly half of our population growth is attributable to immigration. Thousands of busi-

> **I**dentifying change sometimes is like rearing a child and overlooking subtle changes that reshape the youngster.

nesses relocate each year to exploit tax, labor, real estate and infrastructure advantages. The aging of Americans is creating massive transfers of wealth and responsibility.

But discerning these changes is not always a simple task. When you live in the midst of change, it is often difficult to recognize that change even though it has a very real impact on you. It is like rearing a child: When you spend time with the child, day after day, you sometimes overlook some subtle changes that reshape the youngster. Friends and relatives can more readily recognize these changes because of the less frequent contact they have with the child.

Demographic changes may creep up on you in the same way.

They have silently, but certainly, overwhelmed many a congregation across America.

Inadequate Leadership

Throughout this book, I will return to several key themes. One is the extreme importance of strong, visionary leadership in a church. More often than not, the churches that declined found themselves with a pastor who failed to provide effective leadership.

Most people are followers and need a leader to point them in a

---

In some declining churches, a visionary pastor had departed and was replaced by a less-skilled person.

---

direction, to motivate them to act, to monitor their progress and to react to their efforts. Most of the declining churches attribute their tailspin, in large part, to weak leadership.

Interestingly, some of the pastors who led the church to decline were, at one point in their tenure at the church, providing the type of leadership required. However, one of several realities struck. In some circumstances, the pastor burned out and simply lost the will and the energy to lead effectively. In other churches, having reached some level of success, the pastor was at a loss about how to move forward. (This is reminiscent of the Peter Principle: People will rise to their level of incompetence and plateau at that point.)

In some of the churches studied, the problem was that the pastor never was a true visionary leader nor was he capable of becoming one. In other situations, we discovered that the visionary pastor, no longer challenged by the church or tempted by other offers, had departed and was replaced by a less-skilled person.

The loss of momentum provided by the visionary leader eventually caught up with the church, sometimes 5 or 10 years after the departure of the leader, and the church had to undertake radical surgery to restore life to the ministry.

Just like any organization that hopes to make an impact in its environment, a church needs a strong leader to provide direction for the people. The absence of leadership is like a deep-sea diver who makes a dive without air tanks: The diver can survive for a short period of time, but without a key resource needed to successfully accomplish the mission, the diver eventually becomes disoriented and suffocates.

Poor Management

A clear—and vitally important—distinction can be made between leadership and management. It is true that a church cannot function

Management without visionary leadership leads to ministry that is mechanical, passionless, predictable and limited.

effectively without strong leadership. But our research also indicated that many churches floundered because they had ineffective organization and operational management.

If leaders provide the ideas, the strategy and the motivation for effective ministry, managers design the structures, systems and tactics that implement the vision conveyed by the leader.

Leadership without strong management results in theoretical, idea-heavy, pastor-driven churches. Management without visionary leadership leads to ministry that is mechanical, passionless, predictable and limited.

An effective ministry is one that combines true leadership and efficient management and produces life-changing experiences with God and His people. The best ideas and programs are of little practical value unless a person or team is in place to manage these ideas and to facilitate productivity.

Old Blood

How many churches have you known in which young people are virtually absent? It is difficult to build a thriving, vibrant church in which
young adults and children are not a significant part of the mix.

When the church relies exclusively upon the "old guard" to bear
the brunt of the ministry, year after year, without the infusion of
some newcomers, problems are inevitable. The church that either
ignores its failure to integrate new people into the mainstream of the
ministry, or proves incapable of attracting young people, usually suffers serious consequences.

Building Campaigns

From coast to coast, the roadside is littered with the debris of churches that have entered into major building campaigns. "Major," by the
way, is relative to the size of the church.

For smaller congregations, building a $20,000 parking lot could
shatter the tranquility and emotional balance of the body. In larger
churches, adding a $3-million education wing is often the beginning
of the end. The initial excitement generally gives way to tension, pressure and bickering regardless of the scope of the project. An important
reason for this condition is that the fund-raising campaign often converts the pastor from spiritual leader to chief fund-raiser, from teacher
to construction superintendent, from prayer warrior to zoning board
nemesis.

Even in churches where skilled professionals from within the congregation oversee the construction process and professional fund-raising consultants lead the money-raising process, churches struggle with
the dynamics of real estate development. And because a building program often takes years to complete, the shift of focus from a ministry
purpose to a nonperson goal erodes the heart of the congregation.

The Ingrown Family

Declining churches generally focus inward rather than outward. The
ministry that takes place rarely reaches beyond those people who are
faithful participants within the church.

The typical perspective is that the church participants will reach out to help others as soon as they themselves feel "whole" or sufficiently strong to focus on the ills of others. "You can't give to others that which you, personally, don't have to give," was the counsel of a member of a declining church.

The difficulty is that these people become so programmed to focusing upon themselves and worrying solely about their needs and desires that they lose sight of the balance required in ministry.

Many of the declining congregations were virtually unknown within their own community. Because they had committed all of their resources to internal service, people outside the walls of the church were unaware that the church existed. The prospects for numerical growth, much less spiritual growth, are virtually nil in such a climate of self-contemplation and selfishness.

Resistance to Change

Change is uncomfortable for all people because it means a departure from what is familiar and comfortable to embrace that which is unknown and risky. Declining churches often enter their tailspin,

---

Stalwarts in a dying church often argue that things will return to normal if the church can do a better job of doing what it has always done.

---

however, because they lack vision, leadership and a commitment to remaining relevant to their ministry context.

Without vision, there is no reason to change. Without leadership, there is no path upon which change can be managed intelligently. Without a determination to remain relevant (without compromising one's essential values, beliefs and principles), there is no need to reorient behavior to address the needs and desires of a target audience.

In a dying church, change is viewed with alarm because it simultaneously represents an admission of failure and the recognition that the future will not be identical to the past.

More commonly, the stalwarts in the collapsing church argue that things will return to normal if the church can simply continue to do what it has always done but in greater quantities or with superior quality.

Spiritual Health

In declining churches, you find a lack of passion for ministry. Ministry becomes a job or a series of routine activities that are to be performed at the prescribed time by the usual cast of characters like a Broadway play. The people lose the sense of urgency about the calling to serve Christ. The energy generated by the exhilaration of striving to fulfill the cause has been replaced by the comfort and security of habit and routine.

This sad state of the Body is perpetuated by the absence of strategic thinking about ministry, which again is a function of leadership. Without a blueprint to guide the way, based upon a clear understanding of goals and purposes, the church will flounder. And the chances of resurrecting the church by attracting new leaders with a burning passion for ministry are reduced by the reality that activists flock to leaders who articulate vision and plans for making things happen.

Declining churches are generally too immersed in busywork and tradition to concentrate resources or energy upon detailed means of changing the current reality.

TROUBLE BORROWS TROUBLE

As you can begin to imagine, it is rather easy for a church that is slowed by one of these problems to start acquiring other problems.

For instance, it was not unusual to find that ingrown churches also were struggling with poor pastoral leadership. Churches laboring in the midst of demographic change were often plagued by a resistance to change and innovation and were characterized by an older congregation.

The churches that seemed to have run out of energy or that lacked passion often tried to recover from the hardships brought on by their building campaigns...and so forth. The problems can intertwine in a variety of ways and generally begin to feed on each other once the downward spiral gains momentum.

Custom-made Problems
The problems and challenges addressed thus far transcend church size, church age, denominational affiliation and ministry style.

Beyond this handful of common obstacles is a veritable laundry list of idiosyncratic difficulties, problems tailor-made to, or by, the congregation in question.

Some of the unique barriers to church health that our research uncovered were:

- Divisive internal politics;
- Inadequate Christian education and training;
- Dilapidated facilities;
- Frequent changes in leadership positions;
- Pastor-centered ministry;
- Emotional discouragement among the congregation;
- Unreconciled theological disagreement;
- Absence of ministry opportunities for people;
- Financial decline;
- Loss of key laypeople;
- Loss of critical staff members;
- Lowering of ministry standards;
- Denominational meddling;
- A shift from Bible-centered teaching;
- Absence of an assimilation program.

All of these categories include a vast array of distinctive problems encountered by one or more of the turnaround churches studied. Notice that all of the challenges are definable and addressable, but only if the church has the resources necessary to recognize and to confront these ills.

Expect Challenges

The surprising reality is not that these churches encountered such life-threatening conditions. In a culture characterized by rapid and constant change, such challenges to normal operating procedures ought to be expected.

Every organization that works in the ill-defined realm of people-transformation must expect that as humans experience confusion, discomfort and new opportunities in life so will the organizations with which these people are associated.

The bottom-line issue, then, is not whether a church will experience challenges, but how it will deal with them. Without strong leadership charting a course of action with vision-driven responses, the church can count on facing a growing list of challenges, each more severe than the làst.

The declining churches we studied were, as a group, beset by a swelling sea of problems. The churches that recovered from their tailspin were those that demonstrated depth of leadership, spiritual commitment and maturity and the will to perform meaningful ministry.

These conditions resulted in a willingness to reevaluate and restructure themselves within the confines of their theology and values. Sensing a life-or-death struggle at hand, the turnaround churches were driven to renewed life in ministry founded upon an indisputable determination to see the resurrection power of Christ reflected in their battle to regain perspective and influence.

From Dream
to Reality

IN MOST CASES, A CHURCH DOES NOT TRULY FALL APART OVERNIGHT. IN A FEW OF the churches we studied, the decline had an identifiable starting point, such as a major split within the congregation over a particular issue or personality. More frequently, though, the collapse took between two years and two decades to run its course.

In the same way, it takes quite some time for a wounded church to stop the hemorrhage and to regain its health. In the turnaround churches we studied, the time consumed from the bottoming out period to the point at which the church was a growing, functional ministry center ranged from 1 to 10 years. On average, the return to health required an average of 3 to 4 years.

But time was the least significant element in the turnaround. When a church is dying, it has all the time in the world to tinker and experiment. The deeper into its recession it gets, the less overt pressure there is upon the church and its leaders to apply the brakes and to initiate a comeback.

Because it is highly unusual to witness a church that makes a comeback after a steep decline, people find it easier to jump ship and to board another passing vessel than to bail out the one to which they had belonged. Consequently, the pressure to put things back on an even keel shifts from external to internal: A few key people adopt the church as their recovery project and try to nurse it back to health.

ELEVEN ELEMENTS OF REVIVAL

Our study discovered 11 factors that were present when a dying church was restored to wholeness. Although each church implemented these responses in a unique manner, the underlying principles apparently are crucial to facilitating a turnaround.

Naturally, the key to spiritual revival of any kind is the *presence of the Holy Spirit and the openness of the people to the working of God's Spirit.* Apart from this condition, all efforts to influence people's thinking and behavior through ministry techniques invariably will fail.

In addition to the desire to please God through obedience to a special calling to ministry, 10 other factors were present in each of the turnaround churches we explored. These factors may be separated into five categories of activity:

- Relational integrity;
- Strategic initiatives;
- Pastoral character;
- Spiritual practices;
- Resource base.

Effort was made simultaneously by a turnaround church in each of these areas, facilitating a return to balance in ministry.

RELATIONAL INTEGRITY

If a church is to be like a family, and the Early Church certainly provided that type of model for us to follow as portrayed in Acts, it is not surprising to learn that one of the most basic requirements for a turnaround was for *the pastor to establish a bond of trust with the congregation.*

Declining churches either attract the most called and courageous pastors or those seeking a stepping stone to another ministry.

Until the people believed not only in Jesus, but also in the leader He had sent to heal the wounds and to lead the congregation into the spiritual battle, the church would remain a confused, frightened and disunited body of believers. Before the turnaround took effect in all of these churches, the average participant felt alienated from the pastor. In some instances this was a result of frequent pastoral turnover.

Because the church was in a downward spiral, it was an unattractive ministry setting to all but the most called and courageous, or, alternatively, to those people who needed a senior pastorate as a credential on their resume to become a serious candidate at other, healthier churches.

Consequently, many of the declining churches experienced a revolving-door pastorate: pastors working at the church for three months to two years before fleeing to a more attractive position at a more stable church.

In other instances, the problem was not the "who's the pastor this week?" syndrome but the "who's the pastor?" barrier (i.e., having a person who stayed at the church for a prolonged period of time but who had little or no interest in developing a platform for congregational stability and ministry impact).

A typical description of this scenario was provided by one turnaround pastor who described his predecessor. "He had as much church growth background as I do, but he's not a people person. So he was not able to grow the church. People just don't enjoy being around him. I'm a sanguine personality. I'm definitely a people person. That has made a big, big difference."

The difference was manifested in the level of confidence the people had in the motives and potential of their new pastor to truly use his leadership gifts for their benefit. The congregation responded well to the difference, embracing the new leader, slowly at first, but then with relief and anticipation.

Often, the pastors who experienced the decline with the church were oblivious to what was taking place because, ironically, they were too busy performing the ministry activities learned in seminary.

It was not unusual to hear tales of nose-to-the-grindstone pastors who devoted themselves to preparing sermons, teaching Sunday School, performing the upkeep on the church grounds and parsonage and undertaking myriad other tasks that enabled them to be professional clergy but not one of the people. They spent little time getting to know the people or relating to significant groups within the church.

One turnaround pastor described his predecessor as a pastor who was simply burned out after more than a decade of rather impersonal, ministry-as-usual activity.

"My predecessor was a tremendous pulpiteer, but that's about where it stopped," the new minister said. "He was not a people person at all. I think he needed a change. He'd been here for 11 years, and I think he got weary. The people became distanced from the pastor and his wife. He didn't even have a study at the church. He had an office here, but he mostly did his studying and work at his house. He wasn't very available."

In other cases, we found pastors who had a naive faith: "If we just go about our business, God will do His." No matter what type of situation these churches were in, this type of naïveté was not a condition geared to creating emotional and ministry health.

The turnaround pastor, therefore, had to create a bond of credibility and trust within the congregation. The people of the church had to reach a point of comfort with the pastor: He was real, vulnerable, honest, sincere and truly concerned about the welfare and best interests of the people. To build that type of trust, pastors relied upon myriad activities, relationships and techniques, a mixture developed in response to the unique difficulties and opportunities presented by their circumstances.

Pastoral Love of People
Another critical turnaround procedure was for the pastor not only to be viewed as trustworthy, but also to *radically love his people.* Perhaps more than anything else these pastors initiated, this was the element that most clearly reflected the model of leadership provided by Jesus Christ.

"You've got to be with the people," one pastor said. "You can't reach people by hiding behind a wall. You've got to walk slowly

Caring for people doesn't mean that pastors were touchy-feely softies but were in touch with the pain and potential of the congregation.

through the crowds. You've got to take time to get on your knees and look face-to-face with the children and kiss them on their snotty noses. You've got to be willing to stand behind their dad, an executive who doesn't want you to handle him as Dr. So-and-So, but just wants to be your friend for that moment."

As Don Chasteen described the behavior that facilitated a turnaround in a dying Baptist congregation, I was reminded of Jesus and Paul, men who loved the people enough to spend whatever time was necessary just being with them and hearing their mundane stories and mental musings as well as about their pain and desperate needs.

Chasteen said, "I think it takes walking slowly through the crowds. The preacher and the staff, if they don't learn to walk slowly through the crowd and care for the whole family, they're not going to change their churches."

In most of the declining churches, the process of deterioration had been like a Chinese torture test: slow, painful and humiliating.

The role of the turnaround pastor was to be so committed to the people that they recognized his unconventional determination to be one of them, not simply a rescue expert sent to perform a task before departing for a more laudable career in a more respectable setting.

The turnaround pastors had resolved early in their careers that ministry is about the process of being God's agent of love in the lives of people. That did not mean these pastors were touchy-feely softies. It simply infers that they were in touch with the pain and potential of the congregation. They agonized over crises with the people, and they celebrated successes with them.

The turnaround pastor was not a spiritual giant among weaklings; neither did he position himself as the solution to an otherwise baffling crisis and therefore deserved to be looked upon as the church's savior. He tended to demonstrate the same type of selfless love that Jesus had shown to the poor, hungry crowds throughout Israel.

Charles Sundberg said he entered a turnaround situation unprepared for the depth of emotional need existing within the church he chose to pastor. But the need became readily apparent, and his response was a natural but not easy one.

"For a church that has been declining for a number of years, loving the people has to be the number one thing because they have been rejected," Sundberg said.

"When other people leave, they are rejecting the church; so, the people left don't feel good about their church. What my wife and I did was just love them and make them feel good about themselves and their church.

"Now they want to bring people to church because they feel good about it. That couldn't have happened unless we loved them to the point where they felt like we do have something to offer to people."

In effect, what the turnaround pastors teach us is that regardless of the spiritual gifts, seminary training, church experience, natural talents and leadership skills they possess, a key to being effective is to demonstrate love in such a way that people will realize they are significant and cared for in God's eyes.

"All we've got is people," was the way one turnaround pastor put it. "I tell pastors who struggle with turnarounds and want to know what was the magic act that allowed us to grow again: 'You just focus on loving the people.'

"Let the Holy Spirit do the hard work. We're just not bright and tough enough to single-handedly bring about a turnaround. As the pastor, all I'm called to do is to be a channel of care for people who need to feel loved."

Strategic Initiatives

When it comes to the ministry of the declining church, a turnaround requires that certain perspectives and practices be introduced.

Select a New Pastor

The first step may be the most important. To turn around a church, *a new pastor must be brought in* to lead the revolution. Some churches probably have come back from the edge of extinction without a change in pastor. However, we did not find such a church. In every one of the churches we explored, a new pastor had to be brought in to create the climate and plans for an effective resurrection of the congregation.

The reasons behind this requirement are many. An entrenched pastor who has lived through the heart of the decline is unlikely to command the respect and to have the necessary energy not only to apply the brakes to the skid, but also to determine how to reverse the fortunes of the church. The new pastor brings not only a fresh perspective to the scene, but also a different background, a new set of ministry and interpersonal skills and a divergent set of expectations regarding the potential of the church.

Although the pastor in office during the decline may not have been primarily responsible for the negative growth of the church, he is similarly unlikely to have a sufficiently positive attitude toward the people and resources of the church to develop and to forcefully champion a dynamic turnaround plan.

As will be discussed in the next chapter, the replacement pastor cannot be the next graduate off the seminary assembly line; it takes a special kind of pastor to facilitate a recovery.

Release the Past

Ushering in a new leader relates to a second important element in the strategic process of a turnaround: *releasing the past*. While an effective turnaround pastor is cognizant of the proud history of the church, as well as the ills that felled the church, he is not limited by the traditions, assumptions and experiences that make up the history of the church.

A turnaround pastor is one who focuses on the future of the community and the church. While ties to the past may be built, little energy is expended by turnaround pastors in constructing smooth transitions from the past to the future or in making sure that everyone's feelings about the past remain positive and intact.

The future is not won by reliving the past. Turnaround pastors instill in their people an understanding of the limits of history and the challenges of the future. One of the most significant implications of this factor is that turnaround pastors do not pump up members of the congregation by challenging them to produce the numbers that once defined the church (e.g., attendance, budget, Sunday School attendance) or the programs that used to work well.

Instead, these forward-thinking leaders redefined the meaning of success and dared the congregation to push forward toward new and different heights. Interestingly, in some cases, when the issue of numbers of people arose, success had been effectively redefined for the church at lower levels than before. This was feasible because the past was no longer seen as a barometer for measuring success and ministry health in a community and culture that bore little resemblance to that in which the church once ministered.

Define Outreach

Another key, then, is that turnaround pastors *intentionally define the types of outreach the church will emphasize.* It quickly became apparent that, in many of the declining churches, outreach was perceived to be of value, at least psychologically and philosophically. Unfortunately, however, ministry was more of a theoretical construct than a practical reality in these dissipating bodies. Ministry became an every-man-for-himself adventure with little supervision or aggregate guidance over the outreach process.

In turnaround situations, we found that the new leadership instituted a simple plan for specific forms of outreach. Rather than turn everyone loose to do whatever he or she felt was a comfortable ministry to perform, structure, purpose and guidelines were applied to the ministries the church sanctioned and supported. People's energy for ministry was channeled into specific directions; the church's resources were allocated with greater care and precision. The selection of ministry thrusts was tied to the larger vision of the church, and people were assisted in their efforts to comprehend how all of these elements fit into a unified ministry.

Equip the Congregation

Intentional outreach will fail to have a significant impact, though, unless the ministry is undertaken by the congregation rather than just by the paid professionals. Keeping this in mind, turnaround pastors gave top priority to *equipping the laity for effective, targeted ministry*. Indeed, until the people believed enough in themselves as ministers on God's behalf, there was little chance that they would believe the church could sustain a comeback.

In some of the comeback stories, we observed that the pastor focused the people on one or a few areas of ministry expertise based upon the pastor's personal outreach gifts. In this way, the pastor transferred his or her experience and knowledge so that members of the congregation were better prepared to achieve success.

In other cases, we witnessed pastors who identified the lay leaders who could provide hands-on training to equip other laypeople for ministry. These pastors then focused on the areas of excellence of these lay leaders.

Although the methods may have differed in these turnaround situations, the underlying motives were similar: to facilitate ministry by the people, to gain support from the staff and to impact the church by working together for the common good of the target audience.

PASTORAL CHARACTER

As might be expected, the turnaround leader is a different breed of pastor. Although chapter 4 explores the dimensions of pastoral leadership necessary in a turnaround situation, a few aspects are pertinent to this discussion.

Select a Strong Leader

A successful turnaround pastor is a *strong leader*. Declining churches that hired caretakers, healers, managers, administrators, teachers or consensus builders failed to gain ground. Why? Because a church, like any institution or group of people, requires true leadership. Leadership is not determined by the good intentions of the person in charge nor by the title awarded to the head person.

Leadership is the sum of the spirit and activity generated by the person who seeks to do the right things at the right times for the right reasons to achieve a specific, predetermined set of outcomes.

A turnaround church requires a leader who seeks to obey God by doing the extraordinarily difficult work of leading hard-hearted people into God's presence on a consistent basis. You don't move people into the presence of the Holy One by waffling, gently nudging or silently hoping for progress. You lead with conviction, determination, purpose and a plan. In the case of a church, leadership must come from the senior pastor.

In brief, we found that the incoming pastor identified the essence of God's vision for the ministry of the church and articulated that vision for the congregation. The pastor so completely, clearly and convincingly enabled people to see God's dreams for the church, and to believe in that vision so thoroughly, that the vision became their own. Rather than worry about who received credit for the ideas, the turnaround pastor, like any truly great leader, was more enthralled by the fact that the people embraced the right ideas and pressed forward to make them a reality.

The incoming pastor developed plans for how the church would make a transition from its weak state into a more dynamic, influential, attractive presence in the community. The process was neither left to chance nor to others. Without any apologies, the pastor took the reins and called the shots.

Indeed, a strong pastor is not afraid of stepping on a few toes or of

Toughness is a requisite for leadership in making decisions that disturb the status quo but benefit the body.

making tough decisions. Leadership is not about being loved by everybody. It is doing what is best for everybody even though that act may stir up some complaints, disturb some tranquil settings or reshape the world as we know it.

One reason leaders can move other people to respond in ways that are foreign to their most recent experience is because of the energy and enthusiasm the leaders bring to the battleground. Their attitude becomes infectious. Armed with a plan and a positive, we-can-do-it attitude, these churches are bound to experience meaningful change.

Pastor Must Work Hard

Finally, we noticed that all of the turnaround pastors were *hardworking*. Turning around a church in a death spiral is not child's work. More likely, it is a task for a superhuman. But graced by God with energy, passion, enthusiasm, special skills, wisdom, plans and a unique calling, these men and women worked enormous numbers of hours to bring life back into a deflated body. The turnaround process is no nine-to-five proposition, one turnaround pastor confided. "It became my life."

Pastors have different ways of describing their work habits. One of the most unique was portrayed by Gene Wood, who had led the recovery of a Conservative Baptist church.

"I keep very close tabs on my work schedule," Wood said. "Basically, I figure when I get below 55 hours a week, I feel a little guilty. When I get above 70, I feel a little guilty.

"My justification is this. Most people in the congregation work 40 to 45 hours a week, minimum. Then we expect them to be here at the church maybe another 15 hours. So I don't think 55 to 70 hours a week is out of line for a pastor."

Other pastors put their own spin on the schedule required for a turnaround. The bottom line was invariably "40 hours a week won't cut it."

"And tell them, please," requested one leader, "it's not how many hours you put in that counts, but what you do with those hours." In other words, the key is to work smart and hard.

SPIRITUAL PRACTICES

Two particular elements related to the spiritual life of the church were evident in every case.

First, a turnaround church is resuscitated partly due to the *widespread and heartfelt prayer* that is lifted to God on the church's behalf.

The pastor emerged as a true prayer giant, taking hours and hours every week to beseech God for all that was needed in the turnaround experience.

The congregation was led to a place where it, too, embraced prayer as a special, hidden weapon in the battle to turn back the forces of darkness that were pushing the church toward the edge of extinction.

Prayer was at the center of Don Chasteen's renewal efforts at the Baptist church he pastored back to health in the South. He is adamant about the necessity of prayer.

"You've *got* to get people to pray," Chasteen said. "That sounds so cheap. I tell other preachers about this sometimes, and I know immediately they want to say, 'Okay, now get on to what works.' But if you don't get people praying, I don't think they'll catch the vision."

In almost every turnaround church, the incoming pastor recognized that forming the congregation into a team of praying partners would be a difficult but necessary challenge. It may be that the ability of the church to embrace prayer as one of its defining characteristics would differentiate it from those declining churches that never recover.

In Richard Porter's experience at Garland Avenue Alliance Church, establishing the prayer ministry was a risk, but it also was central to the new life he wished to bring to the church. "I really pushed prayer," he said. "I started a Saturday night prayer meeting and said, 'I'm going to be at it every Saturday I'm in town and anybody who wants to come should come. If there's one person, fine. If there's 20, fine.'

"That later became our midweek focused prayer ministry of intercessors," Porter added. "I also went to the governing board and elders and said, 'Would you guys begin to agree with me in prayer once a week?' We do that every Saturday at 6:00 A.M." That choice of time was their decision, based on their schedules, he said.

Often, a distinctive of the successful turnarounds was that people around the world were praying for the comeback of the church. The power of intercessory prayer is an often-overlooked weapon in the arsenal of the Christian. Rarely in my studies of churches have I heard of such reliance upon intercession as a building block in the church development process.

When preaching is unsubstantial, a congregation will become spiritually undernourished and will be incapable of fighting an effective spiritual battle.

Quality Sermons

Another factor in a successful turnaround was the quality of the preaching at these churches. The turnaround pastors indicated, with modesty, that they were not excellent preachers, but that *their sermons were a cut or two better than what the congregation had received in the past.*

These comments were not meant to demean their predecessors but to portray a critical truth: A congregation that is inadequately challenged to know and to follow God's Word is a congregation missing out on one of the fundamental necessities of a true church.

These pastors recognized that their sermons may not have been textbook perfect, but they were generally pleased that their messages were biblical and practical. Although a majority of them described their preaching as expository in nature, this was often viewed as a matter of personal style and seminary training, not as a requirement for a turnaround.

When the people spend a prolonged time in a church where the preaching is unsubstantial, the body becomes spiritually undernourished and incapable of fighting an effective spiritual battle.

Turnaround pastors readily acknowledged that preaching was not the single, most important item in the regenerative process for their churches, but that without a steady diet of challenges directly from the Scriptures there would have been no turnaround.

"It wasn't that I was such a powerful messenger of God's Word," explained one pastor, "but that God's Word was so powerful that even when I was the messenger it shook people up. Sure, I work my tail off to be ready with a well-conceived, prayerful message each Sunday, and I believe God has gifted me for that process."

The fact remains that, unless God can work through somebody who is devoted to the proclamation of His Word in practical and insightful ways, the people will suffer the side effects of being held hostage to the world's views, rather than gaining exposure to God's views. Preaching the Bible is central to every church, but it is an absolute need in a church that is desperate for a renewal.

THE RESOURCE BASE

It is impossible to identify organizations that have been revived from a near-death experience without the presence of a significant base of resources upon which they could formulate their return to health. Churches are no different. The turnaround churches we studied had a war chest of resources that permitted the comeback. Several common elements were found in that arsenal.

Seek Outside Perspective

Gaining an objective, outsider's perspective on churches and church dynamics was a resource common to all but the poorest of the churches we explored. Sometimes this meant attending seminars that focused upon church growth and renewal. Sometimes it referred to hiring consultants to analyze and recommend responses to the existing conditions. The benefit was in receiving an objective evaluation of procedures, concepts and principles that could translate into healthier, more effective ministry.

Interestingly, the names of a handful of consultants who specialize in turnaround ministries emerged on a number of occasions. The tip seems to be that a turnaround church is well advised to not simply retain a church growth consultant but to inquire and to identify the most effective turnaround consultants.

In one case, a denomination has such a valued resource on the payroll; in other cases, the people are independent advisers. The aggregate experience of turnaround pastors suggests that this is such a specialized area of ministry that an "any growth consultant will do" attitude may wind up hurting rather than helping the church.

Staff Support Essential

Another useful resource was *having great staff members* on board (assuming that this was a multistaff church). Often the turnaround pastor would reshape the staff, either in terms of the positions filled, the people filling those positions, or both. When the church was large enough to sustain a budget for staff, merely filling the existing positions was unsatisfactory. Invariably, given the vision of the new pastor and the resulting plans and strategy, hiring new staff people who could faithfully and excitedly pursue the vision and plans was an invaluable aid.

For Bill Barnes, having a group of team players marching toward the same goals was inseparable from the renewal of the congregation. "You have to have staff people who are with you," he said. "They have to see the vision, support you in it and be capable in their own right of doing the job they've been brought on to do."

Leadership styles differ from pastor to pastor, but as Barnes championed the turnaround of a United Methodist congregation in an urban area undergoing radical demographic changes, he found the freedom he needed by being able to trust his colleagues.

"Around here I say, 'Handle it, handle it,'" Barnes said. "I have an associate minister who is responsible for three or four different portfolios. When it comes to those things, I want to know what's happening, but I want him to handle it. I need to be informed, but I have to have others accept responsibility for their areas. You have to have strong staff."

A Committed Core Group

The other irreplaceable resource was *having a core of zealots* remaining in the church and supportive of the new pastor. In most declining churches, the best and brightest people bail out before a true leader can be found and installed as the pastor.

In the turnaround churches, we saw how a small group of faithful participants—usually no more than a half dozen people—remained ready to die for the church. Their commitment to the church and its vision was all the spark of life the incoming leader needed to make the church a force with which to be reckoned.

Because the church is nothing more than the heart of the people that comprise it, the absence of people who have a heart to save the church and to bring it back to a position of ministry prominence is undoubtedly a major deficit if not a thwarting condition.

Other Lessons to Learn

Some clear lessons can be learned from these insights and a few may not be so apparent.

Long-term Pastoral Commitment

For instance, given the fact that a turnaround generally takes four years or longer, the turnaround church requires a *long-term pastor*. In this era in which the average pastoral tenure at a church has dropped to four years, the average is not good enough.

John Bowen pastored the turnaround at an unusual Nazarene church in a major college town. After listening to the stories about the church's 15-year decline that bottomed out with about 70 attending a typical worship service, he recognized the importance of making a long-term commitment.

"In addition to vision, there has to be strong, intentional leadership," Bowen said. "Growth doesn't just happen. And the leader has to be committed. I feel very strongly that it has to be long-term. I have not seen any significant church growth without a long-term commitment. When I came here, one of the things I did was to commit to my people that I would stay for 10 years. I said, 'You may not want me, and you've got the right to throw me out. That's your option. And if you ever do, I'll go. Believe me, trust me, I'll go. But I want you to know that I'm making a commitment to you for 10 years because I feel it's going to take that long for us to accomplish what we need to accomplish.'"

Bowen said that specific commitment has been a very important element in his relationship with the congregation. "I feel very strongly about that," he said. "In order to grow, you've got to make a commitment of time as well as energy and all those other things."

Bowen has led the church for four years, but already it has reversed its attendance patterns and has nearly tripled in attendance. And a number of creative, laity-initiated, laity-driven ministries are operating today, all of which would have been impossible without a new leader whom the people were willing to work with because they knew he would be there for a prolonged period.

The Role of Money

Notice, too, that one of the resources not mentioned as being critical in the turnaround process was a treasure chest full of *money*. Granted, some of the turnaround pastors mentioned the importance of substantial funding in their efforts. However, more typical were the comments of the pastors who said that money would have been a treat but is not really the issue in ministry. They said that when you have the vision and passion to minister, you can either raise the necessary money or compensate for its absence.

The pastor of a thriving midwestern church that had virtually no budget when he took the reigns said, "You know, money can be a crutch. I've witnessed how easy it can be to try to buy your way out of problems. I don't feel having the money is always the right solution.

"We needed money here for a new paint job, new carpets, new desks for the kids, but we just don't have a congregation of means. So we pulled together without the big budget and made some great steps forward by creative resource management. God knows we need more money for staff and other things, but in His time He will provide what we really need, not just what makes life easier.

"I guess I've learned how much you grow when you don't have a quick fix for everything. I know my people better, I've labored with them in unexpected but terrific ways. Money is just not the answer to a ministry problem."

Church Must Recognize Crisis
Several pastors alluded to the fact that, until the church recognized it was in a crisis situation, the necessary degree of change would have been impossible to introduce.

At Calvary Reformed Church, led by the Reverend Mary Fitzgerald, that meant the congregation had to face the fact that the church was on its last legs unless something radical happened.

"It got to the point where these people were afraid that their church was going to die," Fitzgerald said. "They felt they had to grow or it would die."

Similarly, other churches did not take the initiative to make the tough decisions—such as bringing in a new pastor or accepting major changes in the programs and systems of the ministry—until the consensus among the people was that they had reached the live-or-die point.

Unity Essential to Recovery
Finally, a *close relationship between the pastor and the laity* must be estab-

lished. The greatest preacher in the world cannot light a fire under a community simply by the force of words.

The world's most brilliant strategist is powerless without the ability to attract people into the heat of the battle. The most adept leader is just one person among many if the congregation does not follow his or her lead.

Many of the turnaround pastors stated that strong leadership is a necessary but insufficient condition for a revival in the church. A motivated laity working hand in hand with the pastor is an absolute necessity.

Attributes of Turnaround Leaders

I AM NOT A FANATICAL STUDENT OF HISTORY, BUT I HAVE SUFFICIENTLY PERUSED the annals of human progress to know that, for any movement to have a lasting impact, a strong visionary leader must set the pace.

Christianity is revolutionary in nature. The basis of this faith movement is to motivate people to willingly and joyfully accept and practice things that are unnatural in light of the prevailing influences and systems in our world.

Bucking such trends is no small task, which means that any person, group or organization seeking to participate in the Christian cause is expecting something rather extraordinary. After all, the end goal of the movement is to bring people closer to the very being of God by radically transforming the beliefs, values and lifestyles of the individual.

Such a movement, which is spiritual in essence, cannot be sustained without the blessing of God and the power of His Holy Spirit. The model of transformation He provided for us in the Bible demonstrates the importance of His chosen leaders providing guidance to those people called and committed to such a transformation.

The significance of directed, purposeful leadership is readily evident when examining the experience of turnaround churches.

As noted earlier, one of the major reasons for the collapse of dying churches was the lack of effective leadership provided by the senior pastor. Indisputably, one of the primary requirements for turning around a dying church is selecting a true leader who will take loving but firm command of the church.

One turnaround pastor, who has led three congregations back from the edge, is convinced that a strong pastor is essential in the recovery process. "Everything rises and falls on leadership," he said. "If you want to grow, you have to find a leader who wants to grow and who

There's a saying that if you always do what you always did, you'll always get what you always got.

is willing to pay the price. It's going to cost you money, it's going to cost you time, it's going to cost you comfort because you're going to have to change some things. There's a saying that if you always do what you always did, you'll always get what you always got. That pretty much summarizes my experience."

BASIC QUALITIES

Although the turnaround pastors shared many characteristics in common with the pastors who successfully lead more stable churches, they also possessed some unique qualities.

The attributes that turnaround pastors had in common with other effective pastors included the following.

A Team Builder

It is rare to find a pastor leading a healthy, growing church who is not committed to moving the spotlight off himself and onto the people who must do the brunt of the ministry: the laity. This means leading by preparing people to take on responsibility and authority in ministry activity, and a commitment to delegating as much responsibility and authority as possible.

Provides Vision

While it is the task of the pastor to discern and to articulate the vision for the church's ministry, it is imperative that the people comprehend and implement the vision in tangible ways.

When the pastor alone champions the vision, the church suffers; when the people own the vision, the church thrives. The pastor is the initial disseminator of the vision. When the church is truly healthy, the pastor becomes the protector of the integrity of the vision while the people become champions of the vision.[1]

Several of the pastors interviewed were quite forceful in their emphasis on the significance of vision. Gene Wood spoke in such terms. "If we're paid for anything, aside from modeling Godlikeness, we're being paid to invoke a vision. And I don't think the pastor can delegate that."

Wood's experience at Evangel Baptist Church demonstrated the importance of a comprehensive effort to spread the vision among all the people.

"We communicate it symbolically. Where am I spending my time? What do I talk about in conversations? What do you weep over? You have a lot of opportunity to invoke the vision symbolically. And I think we can do so through our speaking."

Wood said vision is discussed several times a year in his preaching and in the church's newsletter.

"I do a state-of-the-church address every year and try to highlight the things I feel are important. We do it through the annual report, writing the vision into our yearly goals. Here's where we failed last year, here's why, here's how we hope to improve it next year."

Every pastor had some pointed comments to make regarding the importance of vision in the leadership process. Robert Thune spoke for most of the turnaround leaders when he not only identified myriad ways the vision is communicated to the people (i.e., through sermons, personal meetings, newsletters, selection of programs, decision-making procedures), but also underscored that articulating the vision is one of the distinctive roles of the pastor.

"One of the main roles of a leader is to constantly talk about purpose and vision," Thune said. "So you just look for opportunities, every chance you get, to remind people what that vision is. As a pastor, I have chances to address groups at different points, so I try to be sensitive to those opportunities and push us to work at being vision-driven."

Grows Spiritually

An effective leader in the position of pastor is one who shuns the spotlight when it comes to personal spiritual growth. The focus in his life is upon becoming a "deeper" Christian, knowing God ever more intimately and being increasingly sensitive to His call, more responsive and obedient to His will. This takes time and effort, but it reaps authentic rewards.

For Mark Bush, spiritual growth is a multifaceted, planned exercise. "I usually go on personal retreats once a month," he said. "Also, as part of my spiritual discipline, I wake up before my family does each morning to have my own meditation time. Something else that's had a real impact on me is reading through the Bible in one year. Mainly, though, the key has been the inner disciplines such as meditation, prayer and spiritual retreat."

An Encourager

The congregation not only needs a leader who provides direction and builds skills, but also recognizes what the people are doing and acknowledges and celebrates their growth. In much the same way that a father's words of encouragement and congratulations can transform the attitude and commitment of a child, favorable feedback from the pastor can make all the difference in the ministry commitment of the laity. And the more personal and heartfelt the words of encouragement, the greater their impact.

Strategic Thinker

Perhaps nobody in the church will see the "big picture" of the church's ministry as clearly as the pastor. Focused by the vision, motivated by the challenge and prepared by experience, Scripture and God's Spirit, a pastor must provide people with the strategic direction and tactical concepts that will propel the church forward.

While the pastor does the congregation a disservice by assuming the responsibility for the total development and tactical implementation of strategic plans, he provides an indispensable service by creating an environment and a track for exploiting the opportunities and strengths inherent in the church's ministry.

Takes Risks

A true leader does not wince at the necessity of change, at the possibility of failure or at the need to take risks. Risks are part and parcel of the game. In fact, real leaders relish the opportunity to take risks because it makes the challenge more interesting and puts them on the spot.

Pastor Mike Khandjian shared the joy of such an experience with this story:

"At the end of 1986, we had a Christmas Eve candlelighting service. Now, they had never done that before and the power brokers of the church got flustered. 'Nobody's gonna come to that, but we'll come anyway.' And I said, 'Who cares, let's just do it.'

"That night, for the first time in our church's history, we had over a hundred people. And you'd see our people setting up chairs, excited, yelling, 'Here comes another one!' These cars kept coming up our dirt road. Our people believed for the first time, 'Hey maybe this thing *can* work.'"

At First Methodist, Bill Barnes assumed a similar boldness. "People don't like change," he said. "There's resistance and talk like, 'We've never done it this way before, it won't work.' The way I overcame it in every instance—and I wasn't successful in every case—was to say, 'Well, let me try it first and let's see if it works. If it doesn't, then you can come back to me and say, "I told you so," and we'll try something else. But let me have a chance to fail first before we dismiss it.'

"When the burden is assumed by one person, then the people can say that it was the preacher's idea, it wasn't theirs, and so it's a little easier to try something. I'll take the risk."

After 25 years in business, I learned that there are very few really clever things out there.

A true measure of a leader is the types of risk that person takes. A great leader evaluates the anticipated risks, considers the plausible outcomes of each and pursues those that provide the greatest potential for success.

A great leader manages risk intelligently. In the process, the true leader seeks ways of being creative and innovative without being novel for the sake of uniqueness.

The effective pastor encourages a wealth of ideas to be created for dissection and eventual pursuit, refusing to be overwhelmed by big concepts or turned off by off-the-wall thinking.

The true leader always accepts the blame for those efforts that fail to pan out as expected and always shares the plaudits with those who make risks work.

A risk-taking leader is one who is humble enough to recognize that he or she must always be a student of life but is bold enough to take swift and aggressive action when the moment calls for action.

John Bowen entered the pastorate after a successful business career. "After 25 years in business, I learned that there are very few really clever things out there," he said. "And I don't have an original idea in my head. I mean that."

How, then, would Bowen explain the unusual ministries in his church and the remarkable turnaround of a church that most observers deemed worthy of a death warrant five years earlier?

"A church can only grow if it has leadership and vision," Bowen said, "but it's a matter of trying to package things that will work and make them happen. Vision is absolutely essential for a church to grow, but I'm also a very pragmatic person."

Turnaround pastors are admired by the congregation for their courage, but their intellectual stability is sometimes questioned. Taking risks can do that; the motives and potential are often misunderstood by those who prefer the safe route.

Yet, the fact that the congregation is aware of the distinctive decision-making abilities of the pastor, and a willingness to go out on a limb for the things he or she believes to be worth the risk, gives the leader a measure of internal pleasure (if not external stature). The satisfaction is especially keen when taking a risk proves to have been a wise decision.

UNIQUE TRAITS

In addition to these common traits, turnaround pastors also possess a few unique traits that prepare them for the world-class challenge of returning vitality to a congregation that is battered and on the ropes. The most important of these special characteristics are described below.

Youth

Almost all of the turnaround pastors assumed the pastorate of their church before they had reached the age of 45. In fact, most of the turnaround pastors stated flatly that, in counseling another pastor whether to accept the challenge of turning around a church, they would advise against taking the position if the person is 45 or older.

The consensus was that the task is so spiritually demanding, so emotionally and physically draining and so taxing on one's family and relationships that only a person of relative youth can succeed.

The turnaround leaders readily conceded that the wealth of experience possessed by older pastors could be a valuable asset in terms of understanding the condition of the church and how to work with people to create the optimal atmosphere for a turnaround. However,

they expressed grave doubts that an older pastor would have a sufficient inventory of personal resources to master the situation.

One turnaround experience often is considered the limit even for those pastors who have been successful in their 30s and 40s.

A number of the turnaround pastors indicated that, while they
had entered the situation in their 30s and were now in their 40s, they
would not dream of taking on another declining church at this stage
of their lives. In other words, not only does it perhaps take a younger
person to create the comeback environment, but also living through
more than one turnaround church might be asking for disaster.

Although we did encounter a few pastors who made a habit of
restoring life to dying churches, even these pastors stated that con-
tinuing to invest themselves in such churches would be foolhardy
after their mid-40s.

Workaholism

None of these pastors was proud of being a workaholic, but most of
them admitted that this was one trait that enabled them to lead the
turnaround. While there were exceptions, we discovered that most of
these pastors believed that a true turnaround requires a pastor who is
almost blindly and totally committed to the task of reviving the
church. A 60- to 80-hour work week was widely viewed as a job hazard
for those called to this line of work.

Was such devotion to the task warranted, given that family and
balance in life generally suffer as a result? The response of these pastors
was mixed. None indicated that he or she was comfortable with the
toll the job had exacted on family life. Yet, none of those who were
workaholics in practice maintained that anything less than total effort
and energy would have enabled the comeback.

While our research did not include a psychological test or profile of these pastors, I suspect that had we measured their personality and emotional composure we would have discovered that they were workaholics by nature rather than by necessity (i.e., the job required it for survival).

On the other hand, many churches that need to be revived are not restored to vitality and are typically pastored by people who are less than totally devoted to the turnaround. As such, one of the unfortunate realities of the turnaround experience is that it may virtually require a pastor who accepts the turnaround challenge as the dominant purpose and focus of life.

Spiritual Commitment

All effective pastors are committed to growing spiritually. However, the turnaround pastors were unusually devoted to seek an intimate relationship with God on a regular basis. It appears that the severity of the circumstances of the church pushed these leaders into a deeper state of submission and dependence upon Him than is found in most church settings.

A realistic assessment of most of these churches, of course, would have led to the conclusion that there was no hope of breathing life back into the limp body. With that in mind, these leaders invariably recognized that the only true plan was to rely fully on Him for strength, wisdom, grace, guidance and power.

One pastor escaped to a hotel room one day a month to read the Bible, pray, meditate and sing to God.

The dedication to an unbreakable bond with God was lived out in various ways. One pastor rented a hotel room one day a month to escape from ringing telephones, urgent meetings and the numerous distractions that comprise the church office. He would spend the entire day reading Scripture, praying, meditating and singing to God.

Another turnaround leader took one day each week to escape the office and to pursue his relationship with the Lord. The application of other spiritual disciplines—meditation, fasting, etc.—was common in this desperate struggle to gain the mind and blessing of God on what the world would characterize as a foolish venture.

A key to the personal spiritual development of these leaders was their initiation of the process. No one had to encourage them to spend more time with God. If anything, their frustration was not being able to spend more time pursuing His mind and His heart. Rather than be dragged down by the tyranny of the urgent, they made their pursuit of God the pinnacle of urgency.

Strong Personality

Most turnaround pastors are self-assured and self-confident. They have to be. The odds on successfully turning around a declining church are definitely not in their favor. It takes someone who does not have to battle with self-doubt to concentrate on battling all of the other barriers to a comeback.

Some turnaround pastors have modeled their careers after what they have observed in the ministry of other recovery specialists and love to tell stories of their mentors or colleagues, including the following:

"Here's a revitalization pastor for you. My friend took over a church that'd been dying for eight years. He went where there were two famous pastors in days gone by, serving there at the heights of their ministries.

"A woman from the church comes up to my friend while he was visiting and says to him, 'You know, if we call you, you'll have some big shoes to fill of those men who came before you.' He looked her in the eye and said 'Ma'am, if I come here, I'll bring my own shoes.'

"It wasn't abrasive, but just an attitude of 'I'm coming to do what God has called me to do, not an instant replay of what happened 20 years ago.' It's an expression of the visionary, forward thinking that's so necessary."

These pastors were not afraid to make tough decisions and to forge unusual trails for the congregation to follow. Often, by force of their unshakable conviction and their winsome personality, these men and women were able to convince a skeptical body to pursue a risky path.

These were not personality churches, but were churches where the personality of the pastor went a long way toward facilitating new systems, new policies, new thinking, new relationships and new directions. Without a leader who was personally compelling, theologically sound and strategically convincing, the church would never have seen the starting line of the comeback trail.

A Potential Visionary

I mentioned earlier that all successful pastors, whether they lead a declining or thriving church, are visionary leaders, but there was a unique element to the visionary activity of the turnaround pastors. These leaders generally had not given prior evidence of being visionary. Although they had exhibited some leadership qualities and had displayed some visionary tendencies, they generally had not distinguished themselves through previous service as visionary leaders.

This research unmistakably shows that it takes a special kind of human being to lead a church out of the doldrums and back to the path of spiritual wholeness. It is my interpretation of the information that people who have strong visionary leadership skills cannot restrain these abilities and must seek an outlet for them. This generally means planting a new church or taking a plateaued or growing church to new heights.

Taking a dying congregation and investing so much energy and inventiveness in a venture of such limited potential is rarely going to be the first choice of a leader with a strong, sharp visionary capacity.

The turnaround pastor, though, is more likely to be the type of leader who has slowly refined his innate visionary skills and sees the dying church as the ideal place to put these faculties into practice. While many of these people might also be drawn to initiating a new church, a significant proportion may be drawn to restoring the heartbeat to a fading congregation.

The Indispensable Quality

For all the similarities and idiosyncrasies of these leaders, the one unmistakable reality is that a church needs a strong leader from the outside to accomplish the turnaround. Some of the turnaround pastors themselves have had to fight their training to diminish the absolute importance of pastoral leadership.

Pastor Richard Germain is an example. "The leader is the key. I used to fight that contention. In fact, when I first sat under Peter Wagner's teaching, I would get so frustrated. I didn't want to believe it. But I've come to realize that if the pastor blocks this, if the pastor is indifferent to growth, if he doesn't have vision, if he just wants to go along, not much is going to happen."

Note
1.   For greater detail on the importance and mechanics of vision in a strong church, see *The Power of Vision*, George Barna (Ventura, CA: Regal Books, 1992). The importance of vision was also underscored in earlier research among healthy, growing churches in the book *User Friendly Churches*, George Barna (Ventura, CA: Regal Books, 1991). Our most recent exploration related to vision—or, more accurately, the absence of it in churches—is contained in *Today's Pastors*, George Barna (Ventura, CA: Regal Books, 1993). The bottom line is that there is no acceptable or viable substitute for the presence of God's vision acting as the core around which a church's ministry is built. Churches that lack a pastor who can articulate and develop congregational support for the vision simply do not succeed.

Strategies
for Growth

As the turnaround pastors will tell you, paving the way for a spiritual comeback in a disheartened church requires serious strategic thinking. Merely wishing that the church will grow is foolish. Doing the things you might do in a healthier church is equally ill-conceived. Even so, change of any type is difficult to engineer. The radical transformation called for in a declining church dictates the need for sophisticated, carefully conceived plans for change.

Turnaround pastors interviewed in this study are not magicians. Like any other leader faced with a difficult uphill struggle, they found that shepherding their people into a new phase of corporate life was sometimes painful, occasionally lonely and always a test of personal faith.

Most of the pastors, however, discovered that their people grew spiritually and emotionally as a result of the process. Typically, not only did members of the congregation uncover some revealing truths about themselves, they also tended to learn the importance of trusting God for their future. For the pastor, a plan of action was essential in moving people to a point of commitment to God and to other members of the congregation.

The turnaround pastors were not all planners by nature, but they were all intelligent and sensitive enough to perceive the necessity of a strategic plan, widespread commitment to the plan and persistent implementation of the plan.

Because every church operates in a different context and has a different vision for its ministry and being, the strategy and resulting plans for each of these churches differed.

Let us take a look at some of the more common strategies (i.e., the direction you will pursue to reach the goals you have set in light of your mission and vision) and tactics (i.e., the specific actions required to bring the strategies to fruition) embraced by turnaround churches. This is truly where the rubber meets the road. Dreams, concepts and theories are made practical through strategy and tactical implementation.

THE PROCESS OF RENEWAL

The turnaround pastors who were interviewed had worked hard to prepare themselves and their congregations for action. They gathered sufficient information to understand their external circumstances.

The bridge between the past and the future is the strategic philosophy that filters ideas, plans and activities.

They invested themselves in getting to know and appreciate the people in their congregations. They had a working knowledge of the trends that would affect their communities and the ministry plans they might develop and institute. They also had a sense of their congregational histories, had taken some time to analyze why their churches had declined and were ready to build on historical strengths without dredging up too much of the past.

Thinking strategically about building a better tomorrow, however, requires much more than understanding past realities and future possibilities. The bridge between the two tenses is the strategic philosophy that becomes the filter for all ideas, plans and activities.

Each of the turnaround pastors developed a clear-cut philosophy of congregational renewal and growth before launching into any significant ministry commitments. These pastors tended to capture the spirit of their people and the heart of the church's call to renewal in memorable phrases. Without trivializing the substance of the task imparted by the phrase, these notions enabled the pastor and the people to take some ever-so-important initial steps forward after years of giant steps backwards.

That is, rather than backing up a car at 40 miles an hour, slamming on the brakes to skid to a screeching halt, then throwing the clutch into drive and jamming the gas pedal to the floor, these pastors determined to made a gradual move toward health by systematically addressing the emotional and spiritual needs of the church in an organized, prioritized, even-paced manner.

Here are a few of the critical perspectives that shaped the process and progress of renewal in these churches.

Be sensitive to the past, but focus on the future. There is no reason to avoid addressing past problems or approaching challenges. Refusal to admit to past difficulties is dysfunctional and prevents the church from healing fully. Refusal to acknowledge a checkered past is an admission that the church has not yet dealt with the real issues that may have caused the decline or the damage introduced by the collapse.

Turnaround pastors led the congregation through a time of acknowledging the past failure, a period of mourning for the strife caused internally among the people and then into a process of renewal that required an admission of the past decline.

This return to the past was a minor but significant element in reshaping the thinking and dreams of the congregation. To ignore the past would be ill advised, akin to having to hide a secret sin. When we maintain such a cover up, we have trouble living with ourselves, feeling as though we have never mastered our circumstances.

The most appropriate strategy appears to be one that looks the past square in the face, determines some of the pitfalls and weaknesses that led to the decline and celebrates the resilience of God's Church toward building on the strengths that remain. There is no health gained by ignoring, rejecting or being embarrassed by the past.

A healthy church confronts that condition, learns from its mistakes and moves ahead a wiser, more unified body of believers as a result of how it has handled past tests and obstacles. What does this look like in practice? The pastor will occasionally refer to some of the dark moments of the church's history without shame, guilt or embarrassment. The people are encouraged to rebuild relationships with those who were hurt or driven away by the events that led to the church's collapse.

The environmental changes that played a role in the decline are reviewed and addressed in plans for the future. People embrace the attitude that this church is a true instrument to be used by God for His purposes as demonstrated by its ability to endure a downward spiral that crushed the structure but not the spirit of the church.

In fact, in some of the comeback congregations, the deterioration of the church was used as a historical marker to remind people that God was not done using them for His glory and that they had perhaps even more to celebrate than many churches that had never been refined and tested in a similar manner.

Spiritual depth has to be modeled for the people. We live in a culture that extols humanity over deity, defines success in terms of tangible acquisitions rather than spiritual maturity and concentrates on maximizing today rather than building for the future. In such a twisted environment, spiritual focus and depth must be modeled for the people.

Americans learn most effectively not through exposure to sermons and Sunday School lessons nor by reading books, tracts or magazine articles. They learn by observing the behavior of others and by absorbing the most compelling behaviors, values and attitudes into their lifestyle repertoire.

This underscores the importance of the pastor's walk with Christ. The lesson imparted to the people was not that God's purpose was to perfect the pastor as a spiritual champion, but to expose these leaders as fallen creatures working hard to become useful servants.

Turnaround pastors invariably described their devotion to God and spiritual growth as inadequate, even by their own standards. They consistently asserted that they hoped their own struggle to demonstrate their faith as a life-changing belief system would quietly influence others in ways that sermons and programs could never hope to do.

How often have we heard stories about the wild, out-of-control children of pastors—the infamous "PKs"—and understood their recklessness to be a bad example to the watching world? In the same way, we learned that the quality of the pastor's entire life had to reflect a deep, authentic commitment to be Christlike at all times.

Ray Cotton has pastored his Kansas congregation for nearly two decades. When he took the post of senior pastor at the age of 23, he had no way of knowing how God would use him in the challenging days ahead. But he always has been an ardent believer in the power of prayer as the center of one's spiritual life.

"If you can find one or two or three people who really believe in the church, you can start out with a small group and start praying together. It can start out like a grain of mustard seed, which will start growing in the life of the congregation" Cotton said.

As an advocate of prayer, Cotton helped lead his congregation into a deeper relationship with God. It was not an abstract lesson from the pulpit, but a shared experience with the living God that built mutual trust and bonding.

Do just a few things, but do them with excellence. The temptation is to try to initiate a recovery by providing a broad-based ministry complete with a plethora of programs and personal services. Having the megachurches in mind as the ideal, a common assumption is that mimicking the structure and variety of these large ministries will bring ministry health.

It is not unusual to find a declining church strive to regain its equilibrium by adding to its menu of ministry options: worship service,

Sunday night service, Wednesday family service, small groups, Sunday School, singles group, young marrieds group, youth program, homeless outreach, community recycling program, parenting seminars, psychological counseling and so on   The typical philosophy of pastors faced with a declining church is that the antidote to decline is for the church to become all things to all people.

The experience of the successful turnaround pastors showed that the opposite was required. Instead of trying to convert the church to become something that it was not by increasing the menu options, they intentionally sought to scale back the scope of the ministry to its essentials. To a turnaround church, small is not only beautiful, it is mandatory.

At the First Church of the Nazarene, Chris Sutherland was able to apply some insights learned from a previous pastorate.

"One of the lessons I learned from my first church was you can't do everything. I think when you reach a certain size, when you get to be one of those giant, colossal [Bill] Hybels' churches, you can do just about anything and everything because you've got enough resources and manpower to do it."

Sutherland attributes part of the turnaround to identifying the church's vision and concentrating on it. "You have to find out what it is you can do and then do it well. We have applied ourselves here to evangelizing and discipling people. That is our focus."

The choice of which activities and programs to undertake was based upon the vision for the church's ministry, the gifts of the staff and congregation, the needs of the target audience and the resources available to enable such a ministry.

The pastor, as the primary decision-maker for the strategic direction of the church, invariably also looked to ensure that the handful of ministry activities undertaken by the church were performed with excellence. This is such a practical approach. Taking on a wide range of programs and services is a sure-fire recipe for congregational burnout.

Because most turnaround churches have only a relative handful of people responsible for sparking and initially carrying the comeback, the chances also are that only a few special talents and gifts reside abundantly among these people. A broad base of programs would set the people up for failure by introducing mediocrity into ministry. Because a significant element in the turnaround is restoring the tarnished image of the church, installing programs that reflect high quality is a critical factor toward recasting the church's image.

In the case of Faith Baptist, taking on ministry initiatives one at a time was crucial. Pastor Doug Geeze said, "You need to infiltrate the church little by little, getting them involved in frontline ministries where they're seeing people come to know Christ."

Geeze selected evangelism as the initial ministry thrust for his new church, which was clamoring for a taste of success in outreach.

"As the workers become excited, they can begin to excite others in the congregation," Geeze said. "It's going to take some time. It can't happen overnight. With us, it was our evangelism program, which

The congregation often is relieved rather than disappointed when the program roster is trimmed severely.

then broadened the church. There may have been other things that we could have done, but that was the one thing we did, and it worked."

Many renewed churches found that people were relieved, rather than disappointed, to have the program roster trimmed severely. People dislike failure. They would greatly prefer doing a smaller number of activities of which they could be proud than offering a shopping list of alternatives, most of which are performed at a marginal level of quality.

Return to the basics. Upon entering the ministry and evaluating the state of the congregation, many of the turnaround pastors discovered quickly that the people were operating in a state of spiritual disarray. They determined that the best tact to pursue spiritual development was to return to the basics and to take a systematic approach in clarifying "what we believe, why we believe it and what difference those beliefs should make in our lives."

The return to basic theology and simple ministry was refreshing for most people, even to those who had been Christians for decades. After a prolonged period during which they had not been consistently and thoughtfully challenged and instructed how to grow spiritually, returning to the basics of the faith was a smart strategy. The people could agree on the crux of their faith. They enjoyed a degree of comfort by returning to something somewhat familiar, eternally practical and encouraging. This step allowed the pastor to restore people's confidence in the core of the church's ministry.

Let the people enjoy some success. The congregation is not ministry-minded first and driven to conduct its other business as a secondary reality. Whether we like it or not, all but a tiny proportion of the congregation is generally wrapped up in the anxieties and challenges of daily survival. Ministry is a rewarding add-on obligation.

Success breeds success; it breaks down people's reluctance to get involved and lures them back to involvement in ministry.

Layer on top of this mentality the fact that Americans avoid situations that pose risk or failure, and you have an unattractive environment to the volunteer corps. How can a leader motivate people to ignore the harsh probabilities confronting the church? One of the key strategies was to develop a few carefully selected and well-designed opportunities to involve people in ministry that are almost guaranteed to result in a positive, successful outcome.

Because success breeds success and because the people of the church are cautiously observing the progress of the ministry under the new pastor, episodes of success break down people's defenses and serve to lure them back to ministry involvement. Just as people eschew circumstances that promise failure, so do they seek affiliation with entities and alternatives that hold the promise of victory. Everybody loves to be associated with a winner.

This approach corresponds well with the strategy of doing just a few things, but doing them well. Excellence in performance of a person's duties raises the chance of experiencing success considerably.

A prime example was a Christian and Missionary Alliance church pastored by Gary Atwood. Located in Salt Lake City, Atwood, an ex-Mormon, leads a church geared to helping Mormons make a transition out of that religion. For months, the congregation had only the pastor's word that the new approaches to ministry initiated at the church were the wisest course. The turning point occurred when these strategies started to reap spiritual dividends.

"People started to get excited when they began to see we were reaching Mormons," Atwood said. "When they realized we'd had two or three Mormon families come in, it kinda shook them up. They said, 'Yeah, we can do it!' After that it began to build. The people began to see what could happen and got behind it."

The turnaround at Evangel Baptist was built around a similar recognition of growth potential. The pastor, Gene Wood, recalled the enthusiasm generated by his people seeing new converts resulting from the church's outreach efforts.

"It doesn't take too many conversions to absolutely renovate a church," Wood said. "We began to go out, taking one or two men with us, and people accepted Christ. We had a baptismal service a few months after we arrived at 13 people. Well, that just does wonders for a congregation! They get excited; they say, 'Well, maybe we can reach people for Christ.' Modeling evangelism and seeing the results made a big difference."

Get a running start and build the momentum. Because a turnaround church requires a new pastor, that person will be watched carefully. One of the strategies that works well for the new leader is to seize the momentum immediately with powerful plans and an active response to the prevailing circumstances.

Check the experience of declining churches that never make it back to health. New pastors who took their time, became acquainted with the people and the environment and eventually announced their grand renewal plan generally found that their ideas and hopes fell on deaf ears and failed to attract the necessary backing. This is often because the timing is all wrong. Congregational expectations are high when the pastor arrives. The window of opportunity for change is at its maximum level. Waiting months before making significant moves may be the safest strategy but is the least effective strategy.

The incoming pastor ought to move swiftly and make a few significant changes. If these changes have been carefully conceived and implemented, positive results should ensue. If that happens, people's confidence builds in the pastor and in the pastor's decision making and leadership capacities. Expanded opportunities for even more significant change are then accessible.

The emphasis must be on people, not on programs. Although the easiest focus for a new leader is to restructure old programs or to initiate new ones, that approach may not be the wisest course. Hiding behind programs can be a trap. The true issue is the heart of the people. Effective turnaround pastors exhibit less concern about programs than they do about the feelings, expectations, desires and spiritual condition of the people remaining in the church body.

Turnaround pastors spend a significant proportion of their early months on the job with members of the congregation. Sometimes these meetings have an agenda related to the church, but often the time is simply spent in informal interaction.

Because it is so imperative to build the people's confidence in the pastor, for the pastor to reflect a deep love and concern for the people and to truly understand where the people are spiritually, emotionally and relationally, there is no appropriate substitute for this type of long-term bonding.

Even after a few months of befriending the people, the focus of the leader must be on tending to people needs rather than on building programs and community services. While such ministry vehicles are necessary and important, they must be developed with the heart of the people foremost, rather than the expansion of the church's attendance or budget as the primary objective.

Help the people develop personal relationships with one another.

Remember, a turnaround church has experienced a steep decline and many people have been lost and hurt in the process. As the new leader attempts to restore the heart of the congregation, there will be resistance based upon recent negative interpersonal experiences, and there will be a natural level of doubt and skepticism to be overcome.

Today, in America, people are losing their ability to interact without the help of some institution like the church.

In America at the end of the twentieth century, we have learned that people are losing their ability to connect with each other without some type of intervention from organizations focused on creating relational bridges. Churches have the greatest opportunities in this regard, but even they must carefully think through and doggedly pursue what it means to be a relationship-driven community. In some of the turnaround churches, this meant addressing past wounds head-on and initiating a healing process. In other congregations it meant working with people to reteach them how to build relationships with each other.

Never let up. This is a long-term process. The people must be prepared for the arduous and taxing task of restoring faith in each other and of revising the public's perceptions of the congregation. It will take much time, energy and money to build a comeback. A critical part of the leader's function is to ensure that people have a rational view of how quickly the church can be returned to health and just how big a challenge they are encountering.

Perhaps the primary factor in this is for the pastor to model honest but unrelenting pursuit of the vision. "Honest" in the sense of allowing people to see that a turnaround is a tiring, perpetual process. "Unrelenting" in the sense of sticking to the task, even when fatigue, fear, lack of resources and confusion get in the way. Naturally, if the leader shows signs of discouragement, the people take it as their cue that additional sweat may not be justified. If the leader backs off from the restoration movement, the people recognize that their continued involvement would be unwise.

Another element of such perseverance is the willingness to take a risk, to fall short of the goal and to continue until the goal is reached.

"You have to be willing to make mistakes," explained Curt Sylvester, pastor of a United Methodist church in the midwest. After the church had experienced nearly a decade of stagnation, Sylvester arrived and helped the church double its worship service attendance in eight years. Persistence was certainly a key in that process.

"We have never had a failure at this church," Sylvester said. "We've had a lot of things that didn't work, but we've never had a failure. For example, our divorce [recovery] group. We had to try three times before it clicked. And we're not afraid to give a funeral to that which does not work."

Programs: The Bane of Renewal

As noted earlier, one of the great temptations is to base a turnaround effort on the ability to create internal and outreach programs. Our study of turnaround churches, however, revealed an interesting outcome: Those that made the comeback had only a handful of common programmatic thrusts. They were more likely to reduce than increase the number of programs.

One program common to most churches was a small group or cell-based ministry. These groups generally consisted of 4 to 10 people that met at a mutually convenient time in somebody's home.

The meetings typically lasted 90 to 120 minutes and were largely based upon relational development. While Scripture study and prayer formed an important aspect of some of these groups, the crucial factor usually was the ability to bring people back together around the Word and the church to create (or perhaps to reestablish) a true community of faith.

The decline of the church usually ripped apart relationships, leaving a number of unrelated cliques in its wake. The turnaround required the rebuilding of true community. Small groups were a common means of achieving that end. While there was some debate about the spiritual character and depth of teaching in these small circles, at least relationships were being developed and confidence in the church was being restored.

OTHER ENHANCEMENTS

No other programs were adopted by turnaround churches. However, other attitudes or strategic notions further enhanced the comeback. These included the following:

The laity had to be carefully trained to participate in ministry. This meant instituting methods for instilling knowledge and skills in the people who made a commitment to the ministry of the church.

The worship services were imprinted with the style, attitude and character of the new pastor. While every turnaround church had a worship service in place, the entrance of the new leader ushered in a new era for the church. To underscore the transition from the old era to the new, altering the worship service—the primary event through which the personality and heartbeat of the church becomes evident—was the fastest and most overt mechanism for sending the signal that the new era had begun.

Creating a viable prayer ministry was common. The ministry not only taught the significance of prayer, but also how to beseech God's blessing on the current efforts of the renewing congregation.

An outward-looking perspective was planted in the minds and hearts of the people. Whether the thrust was local outreach, national outreach or international missions, most turnaround pastors indicated that shifting the people's focus off of themselves and their church problems was a necessary precursor to the people adopting a focus on real ministry.

Events were geared to building public awareness of the church. The objective was to position the church in a desired manner in light of the vision and strategy for growth, and to provide a platform for reaching people in the community who were spiritually unattached or personally needy.

THE GRAND PHILOSOPHY

In the end, these pastors seemed to agree that *what* a church does in the renewal process is not as important as *why* they do it. Timing (i.e., *when*) is not as much of an issue as *how* the task is done. These pastors were less interested in the church doing the work of ministry than in the people being ministers through their lifestyles and values.

The renewal had to take root in the lives of the people who remained as part of the church. That transformation was a critical precedent in endowing the community ministry of the church with passion and integrity.

Potholes on the Road to Recovery

"NOTHING WORTHWHILE COMES EASILY," ACCORDING TO THE OLD SAYING. THE proof of this truism is reflected in the experience of a small group of pastors across America who have defeated the odds by turning around dying churches.

Our research identified a dozen or so common obstacles that a church generally must overcome or work around if it is to experience a turnaround. These barriers to renewal fall into three basic types: barriers related to attitudes, barriers related to resources and barriers related to relationships.

IT'S ALL IN YOUR HEAD

Making progress in a competitive world is difficult. But for a church to gain ascendancy these days is especially challenging. America has clearly entered a post-Christian era. While religion remains important to people, they are not clamoring for the Christian faith, nor is there much hard evidence of people willingly defining their lifestyle and values according to Christian principles.

In this milieu, motivating people to stick to the difficult task of revitalizing a dying ministry is tantamount to inviting a miracle. And yet the truth is that, no matter how charismatic and skilled the leader of a turnaround church might be, the turnaround cannot happen until a sufficiently large and committed segment of people becomes involved in renewing the ministry.

Resistance to Change

One of the most prevalent obstacles to renewal is people's resistance to change. Study after study in the secular marketplace has demonstrated that the organizations that leapfrog ahead of the competition are those that lead their key audiences (executives, employees, shareholders and consumers) to be at peace with the necessity for, and

Introducing people to a new perspective on the past, present and future is required so that people recognize nothing is sacred except God and His Word.

process of, change. The acceptance of new ways for new outcomes is critical to a church comeback.

You probably have experienced the amazing capacity of people to avoid change in their personal environment. If our churches showed half the creativity in winning the world for Christ that they exhibit in the resistance of new ideas for ministry, the Second Coming would be imminent.

The resistance movement may start with the familiar "but we've never done it that way." The battle escalates from there with the excuses becoming more and more creative. People who have remained in the shadows for years suddenly become prescient, able to anticipate looming barriers and problems that others simply are not "gifted" to perceive. Invariably, as the new pastor moves to make his mark on the ministry and begins to reverse the downward spiral of the church, murmurs can be heard that "the pastor is moving too fast."

To successfully guide a turnaround, a pastor must assume the role of change agent par excellence. Guiding people into a new perspective on the past, present and future is required so that people recognize nothing is sacred in the church except God and His Word—all else is man-created and must be treated as fallible, short-term and expendable. The pastor who frets over some internal resistance and delays action until a consensus can be orchestrated is inviting major problems.

First, the delay suggests that vocalized concerns can stop the pastor in his tracks. Second, leadership by consensus is not leadership at all but merely a form of consensus management. An organization is bound to lose ground, rather than to move forward, when the rules of the game are created by committees and groups that must placate every voice.

Small-Church Mentality

Another limitation is the adoption of a small-church mentality by members of the congregation. The assumption is that the church may have to remain small, and that a small congregation is innately superior—or, at least, more comfortable—than being a mid-size or large church. The research we have conducted indicates that this is often a defense mechanism adopted by people who are afraid of failing in their comeback bid.

The status quo is often easier and more emotionally comfortable because holdovers in a declining church may have encountered disaster even when they tried their best. From this perspective, seeking a different tomorrow, even if the goal is to achieve a superior condition, may bring on even greater disasters. What exists in their church today is not their ideal, but at least they know with what they are dealing.

The turnaround, then, cannot take root until the people are willing

to accept the notion that a slice of the renewal effort that "small"
may be beautiful, but "larger" may be just as beautiful, or even more
so. The pastor needs to provide people with a stake in creating a different, larger environment. In offering people the chance to build a
new ministry, they will renew their relationship with the church by
helping to define, create and support a reborn ministry.

Growth Paralysis

The challenges inherent in facilitating this new perspective on ministry requires the leader to confront a common disease that befalls
deteriorated churches: growth paralysis. The problem represents a
vicious cycle that the leadership must aggressively shatter: Because
growth requires change, growth is feared, but without growth, the
church will stagnate and die.

It is a classic chicken-egg dilemma: Which fate is worse, enduring
changes that shatter the personal comfort zone and put the church at
risk, or suffocate by refusing to keep pace with a changing world?

Many turnaround pastors recall the difficulties they confronted in
terms of organization within the church. With the demise of the staff
and congregation comes structural chaos.

Bruce Menning found the internal organization to be a self-creat-
ed obstacle to growth at Trinity Reformed. "It was organized as a small
church and, in many respects, some of the organizational stuff kept
the church from growing," he said. "There were nonfunctional committees, allowing very little congregational participation in the ministry. We had a lot of organizational things to overcome but made
changes in our committees, boards and council to allow ministry to
happen."

As part of the strategic leadership process, the pastor and his leadership team must take an unequivocal stand on growth and pursue their
plan forcefully. People take cues from their leaders, especially when they
model expected behavior and some early success is experienced.

Sense of Identity

This new consciousness about the church relates to the self-image of
the congregation. It is not unusual for a dying church to lack a coher-

ent sense of identity. Turnaround pastors often struggle to understand the church because of the absence of agreement within the body about who they are and what they want to be. The turnaround leader must often define character as well as purpose so that the church can begin to love itself.

The fact that most churches in need of renewal are virtually unknown outside the walls of the church does not help the identity crisis. But this lack of identity allows the turnaround pastor to shape one that is unencumbered by the perceptions of various external publics.

Teachable Congregation
To exploit the opportunity to shape the church, almost as if it were a new entity, demands that the congregation be teachable. Until the people are open to hear what the leader has to say, to consider the directions they may pursue and to understand the reasons behind that strategy, the chances of sustaining the necessary level of support are minimal.

How do you gather a scared and scattered congregation into a body that is hungry for insight and anxious to champion a forward-thinking, risk-taking ministry?

Willingness to Submit
A key precondition is to equip the people so that they are willing to submit to leadership. Until this happens, the church will remain a place of organizational disarray and spiritual suspicion. A congregation must sanction its leadership before it will accept and carry out the steps designed by the leadership team.

Certainly, the act of calling a pastor to lead the church is one step in the right direction. However, the willingness to submit to leadership requires that the congregation have confidence in the motives and abilities of the primary leader (i.e., the pastor).

In an atmosphere of fear, disappointment, self-doubt and skepticism, gaining the confidence of the people is no simple task. This is one reason why the church absolutely must have a pastor who is gifted and experienced as a leader—not simply a good-hearted, well-intentioned, highly educated teacher or mercy-giver or person with ministry gifts other than leadership.

The effective leader will create a team environment, gain ownership of a strategic approach to victory and invest in spiritual development.

Although every leader may take a different approach to exerting that leadership, the effective leader will make headway quickly by creating a team environment, by gaining ownership (as opposed to seeking a consensus) for a strategic approach to victory and by investing in the spiritual and personal development of the congregation.

The turnaround pastors we encountered learned that although the congregation may be discouraged at first, not everyone had totally given up on the church. As long as a ray of hope exists in the minds of the people, the leader has a chance to create the conditions for a turnaround.

But to motivate the people to actively, consistently and confidently follow a new, unproven leader requires an initial demonstration of leadership ability. In other words, a leader earns trust by giving people a reason to trust, by proving himself in the line of fire.

One of the few guarantees available to a pastor who takes over the reigns of a declining church is that he will have ample opportunities to prove his ability to lead with wisdom and impact. Seizing these opportunities and making the most of them will pave the way to gain the people's confidence and to see them join in the church's revival. There are no set patterns on what to do first and no strategies that must be implemented first. It is the task of the leader to take the pulse of the people, to read the circumstances and to make a courageous and wise decision. The ability to do this is one of the hallmarks of a true leader.

THE TANGIBLE GOODS FOR A TURNAROUND

Not surprisingly, a number of the turnaround pastors stated that their job would have been much easier if they had been given access to more money. Surprising, however, were the many pastors who indicated that money was not really the bottom-line issue. The feeling was that, if money or tangible resources are truly necessary, the resources could be found somehow.

Adequate Budget Invaluable

Nevertheless, we did hear from a large proportion of pastors who said that, while money is not the single most important resource in a comeback, an adequate budget is invaluable. Instead of spending precious time developing fund-raising strategies and meeting with people to raise money required to facilitate the comeback, these pastors were anxious to pursue the people-oriented elements of the turnaround.

Raising money took many forms. Some brought in fund-raising consultants to lead the process. A few relied upon their denominational contacts. Others took the parachurch approach of trying to raise personal support money from people they knew from around the country who might have an interest in funding the type of ministry they were leading.

Some of the pastors encouraged the congregation to lead the fund-raising process and made this behavior more palatable by giving the people financial goals tied to expected ministry outcomes. This made the process less money-oriented because the focus was on the ministry purposes rather than on the financial need.

Minimize Focus on Facilities

Some of the turnaround churches also faced problems related to their facilities: their existing facilities were too small, too dilapidated or too expensive. The turnaround pastors typically sought the counsel of people within the church and experts from the outside. Decisions related to facilities are often among the most contentious and emotional issues with which the church must come to grips.

Turnaround pastors found that they were best advised to minimize a focus on facilities and to minimize the financial burden that a church might undertake to improve or to expand facilities. In some cases this might mean selling the existing property and renting a smaller, less convenient facility. In other instances, a pastor may choose to have the facilities improved through a simple paint job and new carpet but to forego the desired expansion.

The wisdom of the turnaround pastors was that the focus must not be on how the facilities limit the people but on how the people must empower each other. Once the people of the ministry are strong, only then will they be capable of sustaining the emotional toll of a fund drive for facility improvements or expansion.

Strategic Plan a Must

It is exceedingly difficult for a dying church to make a serious comeback bid without an intelligent, comprehensive and feasible strategic plan. The pastor need not be the person who creates every element within the plan but must be the driving force behind the plan. It ought to reflect the pastor's ideas, personality, enthusiasm and unique calling to lead the people.

Many declining churches fail to plan for their future and thus watch helplessly as the course of events ushers in greater and greater deterioration. A strategic plan based upon a realistic assessment of the circumstances and vision for ministry is required to break the death spiral.

Some pastors indicated that they created a strategic plan, and even that was ineffective in reorienting the thinking and behavior of their people. Having explored these situations, I have discovered two typical reasons why the plan failed to have the intended effect.

First, the plan was too vague. A strategic plan does not simply outline a series of programs and events that will take place. It is a logical progression for growth, detailing needs related to finances, human resources, space, promotion and how the activity is to be tied to the larger purposes of the church.

Because the church requires specific steps in dealing with the future, the plan must detail how that future is to be created. Broad statements such as "have an excellent Sunday School program, led by teachers who are well prepared and attended by 100 students each Sunday" are more likely to deflate the spirit of the people by raising unrealistic expectations than to equip them to create such a program.

Second, the existence of a plan does not spell immediate and automatic victory. The plan must be aggressively championed by the pastor and key leaders, who then gain ownership of it from within the congregation. Nothing is as pathetic as watching a pastor try to single-

Most Christian churches struggle with the "holy huddle," a cozy haven for those who look, live and think like we do.

handedly enforce personal ideas without the broader prearranged support of the people for whom the pastor is implementing the plan. The key in turnaround planning is a plan that fits snugly with the character, conditions, vision, resources and opportunities facing your ministry.

THE PEOPLE FACTOR

Christ's Church is designed to be in the world but not of the world. It is called to be an influence but not to exist in isolation. Thus, establishing a substantial network of relationships with the community is a must for any church.

Restoring the Church's Image
Having such relational bridges is particularly critical for a turnaround church because these friendships will allow the church to grow, to restore

its level of critical mass, to enhance its public image and to experience the life-changing effect that the church is called to produce.

The ability to introduce new people to the ministry is an important means to instill ministry with a new spirit of excitement and passion. Many turnaround churches struggle initially with this element because the people remaining in the church have been cut off from the rest of the world. Most Christian churches struggle with the "holy huddle" mentality: The church becomes a cozy haven for those who look, live and think like we do. Overcoming the inward orientation of the body is a must if the church is to truly be turned around.

Few turnaround churches found that advertising and other marketing efforts were the key to their reversal of fortune. Restoring the self-esteem of the congregation and their confidence in the church's ministry were necessary precursors to building relationships with nonbelievers and unchurched people and inviting these people to visit the church. It is word-of-mouth, not radio broadcasts and newspaper

Turnaround efforts are severely limited unless the church owns prayer as a world-class weapon in the battle against evil.

advertisements, that brings newcomers in the door. The same relationships facilitated the integration of visitors into the life of the church. The pastor must encourage people to engage in such marketing and ministry activity and to celebrate such efforts.

A Committed Core Group

While the presence of a pastor who is a strong leader is imperative, this factor is not enough to promote a comeback. A church cannot be turned around until a contingent of people is so firmly committed to the ministry of the church that they will sacrifice almost anything for the good of the church, to the glory of God. A strong leader can motivate people to make such a commitment to ministry. But, without a band of believers who will forfeit much of their lives for the good of the church, don't bet on the church's likelihood of regaining its ministry heart and impact.

THE SPIRITUAL FACTOR

It is tempting to regard the declining church as a condition that simply requires a healthy dose of superb technical assistance to correct. Although this assessment is true, it is incomplete. Unlike major for-profit corporations that recently have experienced hard times, the church has a spiritual dimension that cannot be overlooked. Turn-around techniques are useful, but any leader who strives to regenerate a church without placing a primary emphasis upon the spiritual renewal of the body is destined to fail.

The Power of Prayer

One of the most impressive lessons for me was the power of prayer in leading a church through a revival. Simply put, God loves His people and responds affirmatively when their hearts are seeking His and their cries to serve Him with power are authentic.

It is not enough for the pastor to pray fervently, nor is it sufficient for a leadership team to pray ardently on behalf of the congregation. Until the church owns prayer as a world-class weapon in the battle against evil and cherishes prayer as a means of intimate and constant communication with God, the turnaround efforts of a body are severely limited, if not altogether doomed, to failure.

Bible-centered

God seems to react most kindly to the bodies that signal their intentions by being truly Bible-centered. Many churches today seek renewal on the strength of human effort without much attention to the principles and truths portrayed in Scripture. These are bodies that seek to glorify God through style rather than through substance. God, however, is interested only in substance, not the style in which the substance is delivered.

An Outreach Orientation

Similarly, a church will remain in its weakened condition until it becomes outreach-oriented. So many churches become ingrown, wailing constantly about their poor state of affairs, promising to worry about the needs of others outside the church once the church itself becomes healthy again.

One of the primary lessons Jesus taught His disciples, though, was that health is a result of demonstrating love for one's neighbor. When a congregation cannot shift its eye off its own needs and onto the needs of others, it is fatally diseased and of limited use to God.

COMING FROM ALL ANGLES

The wise turnaround leader will not simply expect to deal with a single obstacle to renewal, but will expect to confront a number of them. The turnaround process is so difficult because the comeback battle must be waged at so many levels. Never assume that any segment of the church is sufficiently healthy to ignore in favor of focusing attention and resources on other, more overtly damaged components of the church.

The successful leaders told us in no uncertain terms: Be prepared to address myriad challenges on different fronts simultaneously and even then assume more problems exist of which you are unaware.

As one pastor described his experience, "There's nothing like trying to help a church get back on track to drive you to your knees before God and trust Him for a miracle!"

Avoiding the Downward Spiral

WE HAVE COVERED A LOT OF GROUND CONCERNING THE DYNAMICS OF A TURN-around. The experience of these churches has provided more than just a ray of hope that a decline can be transformed into a serious renewal. Their success has given us the keys to understand what we might do to facilitate a church recovery, assuming God has chosen to bless the church in this manner. Our research has shown that a church may rebound from apparent defeat and once again claim a place of value in God's army.

But questions linger regarding turnaround realities. One such question that has been posed to me as I have publicly presented these insights has been: "What if your church has never experienced a decline? How can that decline be avoided?"

Because thousands of churches every year enter into a downward spiral of varying proportions, this is a reasonable—and important—question. If the decline can be avoided, it is in the best interests of every church leader to practice such preventive medicine.

An equally sincere and significant question has been asked of me in these public settings: "My church already has hired a new pastor who seems to have the qualifications of a leader, and we have been studiously following his directives. It has been four years now and we still seem unable to restore the ministry to health. Why haven't we recovered and what should we do?"

This, too, is a reasonable query because we know that most churches that endure a decline never regain health. It is not because the con-

In most instances, a church's return to health hinges on more than the choice of a pastor.

gregations in question failed to search for a viable leader. No church consciously hires a person ill-equipped for the daunting task of restoring the dying congregation. In most cases, more is at issue than the pastor hired to turn around the church.

TWENTY SUGGESTIONS

Throughout this book, we have identified steps that can be taken to avoid a decline and steps that will help to renew a congregation. Putting these elements together with a handful of other church growth principles we have tested in various churches, 20 suggestions are offered.

Concerning the Pastor

- **Employ and protect a true leader as pastor.**

Little is as important as the quality of the person who leads the church. That person must be chosen by God for the task and must have the gift of leadership. The church must do all it can not only to follow the trail prepared by the leader, but also to protect the leader from burnout.

- **The pastor must determine, own, articulate and unfailingly pursue God's vision for the church's ministry.**

As the primary leader, the pastor is God's chosen instrument to receive and to promote the vision, which is the distinguishing characteristic of the church and the mechanism through which strategy, excitement and unique impact are generated. A church without God's vision is an organization without a valid reason for being.

- **The pastor must model true Christianity.**

All the clever teaching in the world cannot stimulate people to change their lifestyle and values to reflect biblical standards and perspectives if the pastor does not show the people what such a faith looks like in action. If it is not important enough for the pastor to carry out, then it is not significant enough for the congregation to embrace. As the senior priest among the saints, the pastor must constantly demonstrate faith in practice. Actions do speak louder than words.

- **The pastor must create and champion a strategic plan for the church's growth.**

The church must have a course of action mapped out to prevent spontaneous, and in most cases counterproductive, marketing and ministry activity. The growth plan should address the need to grow the congregation spiritually, numerically and in terms of community outreach. Although the pastor should not be the person responsible for implementing the plan, nor for the supervision of its implementation, the pastor is the final point of accountability in the growth process.

- **The people must feel loved and be loved by the pastor.**

A church in which the people do not feel important, nurtured and cared for is a church that is sterile and institutional, not humane and spiritually balanced. One of the marks of the true church is that the people who comprise the congregation feel as though they count, not just as statistics in a head count, but as God's special creation for whom God has sent special leaders to look out for their best interests. The church is not about techniques and statistics but about love, and the pastor must ensure that the people feel that warm embrace as part of God's family.

Concerning the Congregation's Attitude

- **The congregation must be open to change.**

A church that grows is a church that takes risk, and risk requires change. As the world constantly changes, the church must alter its nonessentials to remain relevant and attractive to a doubting world. The process of contextualization demands that the church define the difference between that which is immutable and that which is stylistic and cultural. A church that is closed to change is a church begging to die.

- **The congregation must want to grow.**

Many churches plateau because the people in the church lose their desire for growth. Once the desire to maintain sets in, it is the beginning of the end. This is not only germane to numerical expansion, the concept is even more pertinent regarding spiritual growth and development. A complacent church is one that God cannot tolerate; ask the church of Laodicea.

- **Quality must be constantly enhanced.**

The quality of the ministry is experienced by the world in many ways: the image of the church, the performance of its duties, the depth of the people's commitment to Christ, the condition of its facilities, the abilities of the hired staff, the willingness to try new approaches designed to improve ministry results and so on. Because we serve a God who is excellent in all ways, we are called to serve Him with the same level of quality in all that we do in His name.

- **The ministry must provoke spiritual passion in its people.**

Unless the congregation exudes an intense passion for Christ, as observable in the ways ministry is carried out and relationships are nurtured, the religious teachings and practices of its people lose their power. If the people claim they are serving God out of an intimate and growing relationship with Him, and fail to exhibit a burning passion borne of that relationship, something is radically wrong. A critical task of church leaders is to constantly direct the people into a deeper and tighter bond with God so that their lives reflect a fire to serve Him.

Concerning People's Lifestyles

- **The congregation must seek new relationships.**

A church is built on relationships. Unless the congregation can consistently point to new relationships being developed between its members and those who reside outside the faith community, the church is dormant. Churches tend to recede most quickly when they cease to pursue a high profile in the community through the personal relationships of the church's adherents with those who are not adherents.

- **The church must anticipate the future rather than react to the present.**

Effective churches constantly are taking the pulse of the world in which they have been called to minister. They respond by sensing the coming realities and by preparing to meet them head on. The church that waits for the future is the church that ceases to be relevant to the world. The future belongs to those who create it. God has called His people to master the world by creating the future, through His power, for His glory and according to His purposes.

- **The laity must be meaningfully motivated and equipped for ministry.**

A ministry that is conducted solely by the pastor is not a church. A church in which the people minister without adequate encouragement or preparation and support is a weak vessel and one that will burn out quickly. For a church to have a lasting, positive impact, the people must have their gifts recognized and honed, and opportunities for applying these gifts must be developed and encouraged.

- **When people perform true ministry, they should be applauded.**

A successful ministry is one in which people are recognized for their accomplishments, not to place someone on a pedestal, but because human beings need to be recognized for their good works. These works do not guarantee a place in heaven, but they do have a positive effect on the lives of the people, on those who minister alongside of these people and on the lives of those touched by the good works. Put in proper perspective, a bit of celebration and appreciation regarding true ministry can help maintain an active and happy congregation.

- **The emphasis must be on outreach.**

God did not call us to focus on our needs but on the needs of others. By becoming less egocentric and more other-centered we become more Christlike and His church becomes more healthy. Inreach has a place in ministry, but that place is secondary to outreach.

The Church's Faith and Resources

- **Prayer must permeate the ministry.**

A healthy church is a praying church as determined by the number of people who pray, the frequency with which they pray, the intensity with which they pray and the joy they experience from their prayers. If God is really believed to be the power source and prayer is really seen as our means of communication with Him, a church's faith can be determined by the condition of its prayer life.

- **The church staff must be superb.**

Working for a church is not just a job, it is a divine, special calling. The people ministering through a church as staff people (ordained or not) must give evidence of the privilege of professional ministry and the fruits of their labors. A church with a staff that is anything less than a united, high-quality, high-impact team is a church vulnerable to decline.

- **The church learns from objective sources.**

Self-reliance regarding the assessment of ministry purity, productivity and planning is a ticket to oblivion. Because insiders cannot be objective in their evaluation of the church, it is invaluable to seek and to consider the views of experts who can offer a unique perspective. Outsiders also can supply creative ideas that might never arise from insiders. Too much isolation can be damaging.

- **The church must establish means of monitoring its ministry health on a consistent basis.**

A church that fails to evaluate its activity is a church clamoring for sloppy ministry and declining standards of influence. A variety of criteria of ministry success must be determined and tracked over time, allowing the church to study its ministry objectively.

- **The church must enter into a building campaign with extreme care.**

It may be better not to build bigger, newer or differently located facilities than to undertake a major building campaign. Any church that engages in such a campaign must do so with tremendous caution and sophistication. It also must be prepared to lose its pastor within five years of the campaign's completion.

- **The church must maintain a standard of strong, practical Bible teaching.**

People need to be spiritually challenged, instructed and refreshed, which is the job of the church. If any purposes or philosophies undermine the unapologetic, consistent teaching of God's Word in ways that transform people's lives, the church is headed for a fall.

The church that has these elements in place is less prone to a collapse than are churches that are not as well balanced. Because we are dealing with spiritual forces that are powerful, unseen and uncanny in their cleverness, it is impossible to fully protect against a decline. But, based on what current research has indicated, the church that has covered these 20 bases is well on its way to a long stretch of healthy ministry.

CONFRONTING DECLINE

Many churches in America have experienced the death spiral and have bottomed out, hoping that the arrested decline would bring with it a chance to reverse the church's recent fortunes and to recover, only to discover that such growth did not occur.

Other churches have experienced the decline and have brought in a new pastor, one with many leadership qualifications, only to witness a continuation of the rapid demise. What does this mean for these churches? While every case must be studied and dealt with as a unique situation, several responses cover a range of situations.

Some Churches Cannot Be Revitalized

Undoubtedly some churches have run their course and can be closed down permanently. Some churches cannot be resuscitated because they lack a strong leader, others because they do not have the indigenous core of zealots who can serve as the spark through which the ministry will be reignited.

Any church engaged in God's work will leave its mark on people who minister while it is alive.

In some cases, it appears that no need exists for the church to continue because other ministries in the area are performing the same tasks more effectively. Sometimes, the environment has changed significantly enough so that the ministry that had been the heart of the church is no longer viable. The tough truth is that in certain circumstances it is simply best to let a church become a positive part of history.

If the church has truly engaged in God's work, it will have left its mark on the people who experienced the ministry while it was alive. These people become the ministry legacy of the church, using what they learned and experienced through the church in other ministry settings and situations.

The determination to close a church is not a sign of weakness, but a sign of courage and faith. Like an aged athlete who ponders the proper time to retire, a church that considers its options must remember that the goal is not longevity but effective, pure-hearted service.

Calling it quits after a season of faithful service is not a disgrace. Disgrace only occurs in refusing to do what is best for God's kingdom, which may mean releasing people to work through and to interact with other ministries.

Indeed, closing a church does not indicate that it failed, any more than the death of an elderly human being suggests that the person lived a useless life. Indeed, if eternal tangible presence of a ministry is the key criterion for success, we would have to judge the life of Christ to have been a failure. And based on all we know and believe, that would be a foolish conclusion to draw.

One turnaround pastor summarized his 40 years of ministry experience and observations by saying, "No, every church cannot be turned around. Some are full of emotionally crippled people. We spend far too much time trying to renew churches that can't be renewed. We should just leave them alone and start another church full of people who want to grow. Don't kill the old church. It'll run down and kill itself over time. It's much easier to start a live church than to renew a dead one, and much more productive in the end."

Richard Germain concurred. "Not every church can be turned around. I've watched a lot of guys break their hearts trying. Sometimes it just doesn't happen, and I don't understand all the reasons why. But I do know that some specific circumstances and resources, in addition to the working of the Holy Spirit, have to be there."

Pastoring a turnaround church takes such a personal toll that successful leaders seldom revive more than one or two churches during a career.

The Leader Must Be Unique

Not every pastor who is truly a leader is qualified or skilled to be a turnaround pastor. As was discussed in chapter 4, a turnaround pastor is a truly unique human being, skilled in ways that are uncommon even among the ranks of the best-known and most talented clergy. Being a visionary leader is not, by itself, sufficient to prepare a person to lead a dying church back to health.

Although we do not have quantitative evidence to support this assertion, it appears that relatively few leaders currently serving the church are truly turnaround pastors. And because of the enormous personal toll the turnaround process takes on people, even these individuals are likely to revive only one or two churches during their ministry careers. Thus, the chances of finding a turnaround pastor are slim.

The $64,000 Question

Perhaps we now can begin to understand why more churches do not recover from a serious decline. On the one hand, we know that as the life-cycle theory shows us, every organization has a natural life span. While that life may be prolonged or extended through certain creative leadership practices by unusually gifted leaders, these circumstances are the exception to the rule.

The typical organization will die after a certain period of time. On the other hand, we also know that relatively few people are so uniquely gifted—and, in the case of a church, are called—that they can lead a successful comeback effort.

All things are possible with God. But that does not mean all of the things we hope for are likely.

The Last Hurrah

In looking back on what we discovered from interacting with the turn-around churches, several additional observations may be of benefit as you learn from the experience of the special churches included in this study.

THE USER FRIENDLY QUOTIENT

In an earlier study, which was released as *User Friendly Churches*, I found that many of the churches that are having the desired impact on people's lives for God's glory have adopted a style of thinking and behaving that sets them apart. To convey the notion of ministry that is contextualized, we employed the adjective "user friendly." This expression does not connote any form of spiritual compromise, which would not please God, nor indicate a genuine Christian ministry. The term reflects the steadfast determination of these churches to remain theologically pure while adapting their ministry methods to the needs of the audience and to the tenor of the culture.

Turnaround churches appear to be ministries that embrace a user friendly approach to ministry. While these churches may not be sufficiently active nor healthy enough to sustain the full range and depth of ministry found at the prototypical user friendly churches, the turnaround bodies are clearly congregations that have enveloped the mind-set and practices of the esteemed, user friendly churches of the nation.

This characterization also suggests that turnaround churches remain in a state of metamorphosis: Their recovery, though easily discernible, is not yet complete. In fact, much like a person recovering from an addiction, the recovery may never be complete, but always in process. The encouraging fact is that these are congregations that have reconfigured not only their structure but also their attitudes, their goals and their ministry practices toward maximizing their ministry impact.

THE KEY QUESTION

Another reality that should not be overlooked is that many of the turnaround pastors we interviewed had a variety of offers for employment. The church they eventually helped turn around was not the only opportunity they had under consideration. They were not men and women who were simply desperate for a full-time ministry position and thus had to take the only offer on the table.

What is especially intriguing, though, is *why* these men and women chose to accept a leadership position in circumstances from which most pastors would run. The decision to pastor the crisis church was made after answering a critical question: not "how can this church be turned around?" but "should this church be resurrected?" The focus was upon making sure that the church truly played a part in God's redemptive plan.

A church turnaround can be attempted on the basis of human ego ("I can really make something of this church and establish a name for myself while doing something good for the people as well"), or on God's vision ("He wants this church to continue, in strength, for His specified purposes, and I sense that I have been chosen to lead this church, to show His power and love").

It appears that turnaround pastors typically accept such an opportunity only after they are convinced that the position is not simply a chance to prove their leadership abilities, but is a response of obedience to a unique (if scary) call from God based upon His desire to revitalize the church.

MINISTRY EQUILIBRIUM

Our research also underscored the importance of *balance* in ministry. Studying comeback congregations taught, once again, that a sound church is one that recognizes and intentionally strives to achieve balance in spirituality (i.e., theology and ministry activity), methodology and heart. Allowing one of these components to overshadow the others serves to undermine the aggregate potential and impact of the church.

Most churches have a natural strength in one of the three areas. To achieve balance among them, a church must consciously initiate

Influencing the heart dimension of people cannot be facilitated by structures, procedures and personality attributes.

efforts to upgrade the other elements of the ministry without permitting the ministry to suffer from the decision, not simply to proceed full tilt in its area of strength. The most appropriate strategic approach, of course, is to market your strengths while minimizing (and enhancing) your weaknesses. But this must be done in the context of striving for balance.

My assessment is that it is often easiest to find or to create strengths in the areas of methodology and spirituality. The toughest dimension to improve is the heart of the congregation, for this is where the real battle for people's lives takes place.

You can read about methods of outreach and can create programs and systems that will allow the church to make headway. You can teach and preach biblical truth and principles, and can develop ministry programs and services that provide authentic and challenging Christianity. But influencing the real motivations and emotions of people—the heart dimension—is something that cannot simply be facilitated by structures, procedures and personality attributes. Facing the tough task of bringing people's hearts into alignment with the character and purposes of Christ is a critical challenge affecting the comeback potential.

THE IRREPLACEABLE FACTOR

As our studies consistently note, there is *no substitute for strong leadership*. I am absolutely convinced that, had lesser individuals been placed in charge of the ministry of these dying congregations, they would not have become focal points for our study. These churches were enabled to recover from their past and present traumas because they had individuals with strong, visionary leadership skills committed to using every ounce of strength and every shred of intellect to help the church regain its spiritual health.

Most church plants never really get off the ground because they do not have an appropriate spiritual leader. A large proportion of the nation's established churches are not making a difference in people's lives because they lack the spiritual leadership required to front such a movement of transformation. And most declining churches never return to health because they have well-intentioned but ill-chosen people directing the comeback effort.

A turnaround pastor is an unusual type of leader, and most crisis congregations do not have such a leader in the pastorate. These people make the right decisions for the right reasons. They are able to design a plan for the comeback that makes sense and that people will accept. They are capable of motivating people who would otherwise allocate their resources to other ventures.

This is not to suggest that anything other than God's blessing is at the core of the turnaround. However, to funnel that blessing in appropriate ways to the people whom God has called to be His agents of transformation, the pastor plays an incredibly important role.

GOOD, BAD, BETTER, BEST

In summary, the good news is that a Christian church can recover its health and spiritual impact even after a "spectacular" debilitating collapse.

The bad news is that the odds of experiencing such a turnaround are slim.

But there is even better news than the fact that a turnaround is possible. We now know enough about congregational dynamics to state that the best way to be turned around is to avoid the need for a turnaround. We can now identify the critical steps a church may take to preclude the necessity of being turned around from the brink of extinction.

But the best news of all is that God is in control. The humility of John Bowen was well captured when he described his insights into what had enabled his understaffed, underfunded, space-poor, numerically depleted church to be restored to vitality. "The other day a fellow asked me, 'How in the world can you grow a multiethnic church and how in the world did you do it?' And I said, 'You know, that's a great question. It beats me!' I don't know if I could give you one good insight into how to do it. I really, deeply, honestly in my heart cannot say that I am doing this. It's just happening.

"We do some things that facilitate it, and some things that don't seem to work too well....We got our vision three years ago, and the vision is everything....You really have to believe that God has called you to this, and that it really is His ministry. The things you're involved in can be so overwhelming that if you try to handle them on your own, you would be devastated."

Is Bowen, perhaps speaking on behalf of his fellow turnaround pastors, simply a modest leader? Or did he, perhaps, happen to be in the right place at the right time to receive human credit and notoriety for the recovery of his church? Or maybe he and his colleagues who have been instrumental in the turnaround process have relied upon

The experience of pastors who have helped turn around a church is that God, and God alone, is in control.

the best of human insight and techniques to cause the turnaround, but cloak their efforts in the religious talk and self-deprecating manner that is expected of them.

Hardly. These are people who have been called by God to fulfill a very special, highly unusual and unique function. Their humility is real—just as real as that of the heart surgeon who performs the proper techniques during a heart transplant but acknowledges afterwards that he simply does not possess the power or the skill to ensure that the operation would be a success.

The experience and exhortation of those who have successfully come through a turnaround is that God, and God alone, is in control. If we truly seek His will and submit to His plans, we will not only experience His best for our lives, but also will enjoy the process of ministry.

Even for the renowned champions of ministry whose lives are enshrined for us in the pages of the Bible, ministry was often challenging and wearying. But when we are truly in sync with Him, ministry can be transformed from an anxiety-producing duty to spirited and victorious service.

Appendix

This book is based on interviews with 30 pastors who led churches through the turnaround process. Each of them has given us permission to use the information they provided. The following information is provided to help readers understand the types of people and churches represented in this study. To protect these gracious people from the typical barrage of requests for information and to prevent the travesty of ministry by mimicry, some background information has been excluded.

CHANGES IN ATTENDANCE

In some churches, reliable records were not available to provide a completely accurate understanding of the change that had taken place in worship service attendance at the church. Excluding those congregations that did not have complete and reliable records, here is a recount of the attendance patterns at the churches studied.

High Point	Low Point	Current Attendance
133	43	135
70	45	150
150	75	174
220	70	200
180	160	250
307	154	290
350	180	310
200	120	345
610	380	536
550	350	560
400	215	600
425	335	740
310	160	800
700	325	2,300
2,100	1,300	3,300
400	250	2,200

REPRESENTATION

In total, of the 30 cases studied, 14 denominations are represented. They are:

Christian Church
Christian and Missionary Alliance
Church of God, Anderson
Church of the Nazarene
Conservative Baptist
Evangelical Free
Evangelical Presbyterian Church
Lutheran Church—Missouri Synod

Presbyterian Church in America
Presbyterian Church, U.S.A.
Reformed Church in America
Southern Baptist Convention
United Church of Christ
United Methodist Church

In addition, we spoke with pastors who led churches through the turnaround process in 16 states. These states are spread across each of the major regional divisions identified by the Census Bureau.

THE PASTORS WHO LED THE TURNAROUND

Our deepest thanks are extended to the following pastors and to their churches for sharing insights with us regarding their experience, and for their commitment to make their church a solid and effective expression of the love, power and ministry of Jesus Christ.

Gary Atwood, Salt Lake Alliance Church
Bill Barnes, First United Methodist Church
John Bowen, Cambridge Church of the Nazarene
Joe Bubar, Bethany Evangelical Free Church
Mark and Miriam Bush, Covenant Community Church
Michael Cassara, Bethany Church of Christ
Don Chasteen, Ridgecrest Baptist Church
Ray Cotton, Central Community Church
Tim Feather, Simpson Memorial Church
Mary Fitzgerald, Calvary Reformed Church
Doug Geeze, Faith Baptist Church
Richard Germain, First Congregational Church
Don Giesmann, First Presbyterian Church
Dennis Johnson, Eaton Evangelical Free Church
Mike Khandjian, Wildwood Presbyterian Church

Bruce Larson, University Presbyterian Church
Bruce and Vicki Menning, Trinity Reformed Church
Bud Parrish, Lankford Memorial Baptist Church
Richard Porter, Garland Avenue Alliance Church
T. Wayne Price, Rose Hill Baptist Church
Harry Reeder, Christ Covenant Presbyterian Church
Doug Rumford, First Presbyterian Church
Ted Sauter, First United Methodist Church
Charles Sundberg, Austin First Church of the Nazarene
Chris Sutherland, Covington First Church of the
    Nazarene
Curt Sylvester, St. Joseph's United Methodist Church
Robert Thune, Christ Community Church
Steve Wagner, Prince of Peace Lutheran Church
Jon Wilson, LaHabra Hills Presbyterian Church
Gene Wood, Evangel Baptist Church

Barna Research Group
L i m i t e d

OTHER RESOURCES FROM GEORGE BARNA AND THE BARNA RESEARCH GROUP, LTD.

Founded in 1984, the Barna Research Group, Ltd. exists to provide current, accurate and reliable information to Christian leaders so they can make better ministry decisions. Toward that end, the company produces numerous published resources to assist church leaders. A sampling of those are listed below:

Newsletter

- *Ministry Currents*, a quarterly newsletter containing the latest information and trends analyzed by Barna Research for the practical benefit of church leaders.

Books by George Barna

- *Absolute Confusion—The Barna Report Volume 3, 1993-94,* Regal Books, 1993

- *Today's Pastors*, Regal Books, 1993
- *The Future of the American Family*, Moody Press, 1993
- *Finding a Church You Can Call Home*, Regal Books, 1992
- *The Power of Vision*, Regal Books, 1992
- *The Invisible Generation: Baby Busters*, Barna Research Group Books, 1992
- *The Barna Report 1992-93*, Regal Books, 1992
- *A Step-by-Step Guide to Church Marketing*, Regal Books, 1992
- *What Americans Believe*, Regal Books, 1991
- *User Friendly Churches*, Regal Books, 1991
- *The Frog in the Kettle*, Regal Books, 1990

Reports

- *Unmarried America*, 1993
- *Never on a Sunday: The Challenge of the Unchurched*, 1990
- *Sources of Information for Ministry and Business*, 1992

For further information on these and other resources, or on Barna Research seminars on cultural trends and current ministry, write to:

Barna Research Group, Ltd.
P.O. Box 4152
Glendale, CA 91222-0152